A Simple Guide
To Fabulous Photography

For Beginners

By
Rex Lee Reynolds

A SIMPLE GUIDE
TO FABULOUS PHOTOGRAPHY

FOR BEGINNERS

ISBN: 978-0-557-35135-0

A Simple Guide To Fabulous Photography

Table Of Contents

Forward _____ 6

Dedication _____ 8

CHAPTER ONE _____ 9

The Basics _____ 9

What Kind Of Camera Should You Use? _____ 9

Four Basic Steps For Good Shots_____ 10

Lighting _____ 11

Get Close Enough To Your Subject _____ 14

Keep Distractions Out Of Your Shot _____ 14

Red Eye Removal _____ 17

More Subtle Distractions _____ 17

Make Sure Your Subjects Are Well Rested _____ 17

Make Sure Your Subjects Are Not Hungry _____ 17

Take A Good Number Of Shots Of The Same Scene_____ 19

CHAPTER TWO _____ 21

Shooting Indoors _____ 21

Consider Indirect Lighting _____ 21

Night Photography_____ 22

Should You Use A Tripod?_____ 24

CHAPTER THREE _____ 26

Tips For Working With Your Photo Files _____ 26

Be Sure To Backup Files _____ 26

External Disc Drives & Hard Drives - Advantages _____ 26

Renaming Touched Up Files _____ 27

Tips For Equipment Care _____ 28

Photography Widows _____ 28

No Swimming _____ 28

No Smoking _____ 28

No Radiation _____ 29

CD/DVD Drives _____ 29

Batteries & Video Tapes _____ 29

Tape Re-winder? _____ 29

Do You Have A Strap For That? _____ 30

Chapter Four _____ **31**

Self Portraits _____ 31

Re-Touching _____ 32

Let Your Camera Do Most The Work _____ 33

One Step Photo Fix _____ 34

Smart Photo Fix _____ 35

CHAPTER FIVE _____ 36

Video Photography _____ 36

Introduction _____ 36

Video Uses _____ 37

Video Basics _____ 38

Camcorder Settings_____ 39

Lighting Check _____ 39

Extra Photo Lights - Floodlights_____ 40

Sound Check _____ 41

Microphones _____ 42

CHAPTER SIX _____ **43**

Video Editing Software_____ 43

CHAPTER SEVEN _____ **48**

Aerial Photography – Can You Imagine? _____ 48

CHAPTER EIGHT _____ **52**

The Joys Of A Telephoto Lens_____ 52

CHAPTER NINE _____ **57**

Should I Become A Professional?_____ 57

Legal Matters _____ 58

About The Author _____ **61**

Other Books By Rex Lee Reynolds _____ **62**

Index_____ **63**

Forward

Having enjoyed photography since I was a young child with an inexpensive eight-dollar camera I got from a greeting card company as my payment for selling a few boxes of their Christmas cards, I found myself enthusiastically stepping into that magical world so many of us have enjoyed, with the experience of looking through a viewfinder, pressing a button and capturing a moment in time that will last forever. Since those fun filled days I have continued the adventure for many years with just as much if not more excitement and pleasure from each shot as I had experienced with the first.

Advancements in photo technology found me continuing my adventures and eventually filming and photographing some of the most beautiful people in the world as a professional photographer. And whether pushing that button as a professional or just for fun the excitement just never becomes any less.

If you are like me you love taking pictures and probably take quite a lot of them, and you've probably been doing it since you were a little kid. With the coming about of the really fancy cameras things can get confusing as to what settings to use to get this shot or that one, and the idea here is to simplify the process as much as possible so you can get the best photos with the least amount of time spent on learning how to do it.

As a professional photographer my photos have been mostly of models and actors to help them find work, in addition to various kinds of aircraft and outdoor scenery that I have enjoyed filming and photographing very much. But whether you are taking a photo of a person, landscape, action shot or whatever, the basic principles are the same no matter what subject is being used for the shot.

There is probably nothing terribly wrong with the shots you are already taking. They may very well be quite good but you are obviously interested in taking them to the next level of perfection, otherwise you wouldn't be reading this. As you will see it doesn't have to be complicated. Whether you are using a simple camera or a very expensive one with all the fancy extras, the principles are the same for taking good shots that will completely amaze people and get you a lot of nice compliments.

And there is no reason for us to get too serious about it. In the old days they had debtor prisons where they would send people who didn't pay their light bill. They don't do that anymore, and if we talked to everyone who is in prison now and asked them what they are in for, we probably wouldn't fine too many that would tell us they are there for taking bad pictures.

Disclaimer

The author, publisher and distributors of this book will in no manner whatsoever assume any responsibility, or liability of any kind for advice or methods provided in this book and used by the reader of this book. The reader assumes all responsibility and liability for his or her actions, as a result of reading this book and using ideas found herein.

In a number of places advice and/or recommendations are given regarding particular companies and their services, and I would like to state that I am in no way employed by any of the companies or services being recommended or suggested, or being paid any fees of any kind for mentioning these companies and their services.

No warrantees or guarantees of any kind are being made or implied by the author or publisher as to the reliability or soundness of any of these companies or services being mentioned or recommended. No liability of any kind whatsoever is or will be assumed by the author or publisher.

Dedication

This book is dedicated to my good friend Sophia, an absolute angel from the very heart of heaven, who makes people so happy just by being near them, and one of the most beautiful people this world has been fortunate enough to be graced with, for her never-ending kindness and support through the years, an amazing and most beautiful person inside and out, who has been a constant source of inspiration, in helping me immensely in my attempts to capture and behold all the most incredible natural beauty wherever I am able to find it.

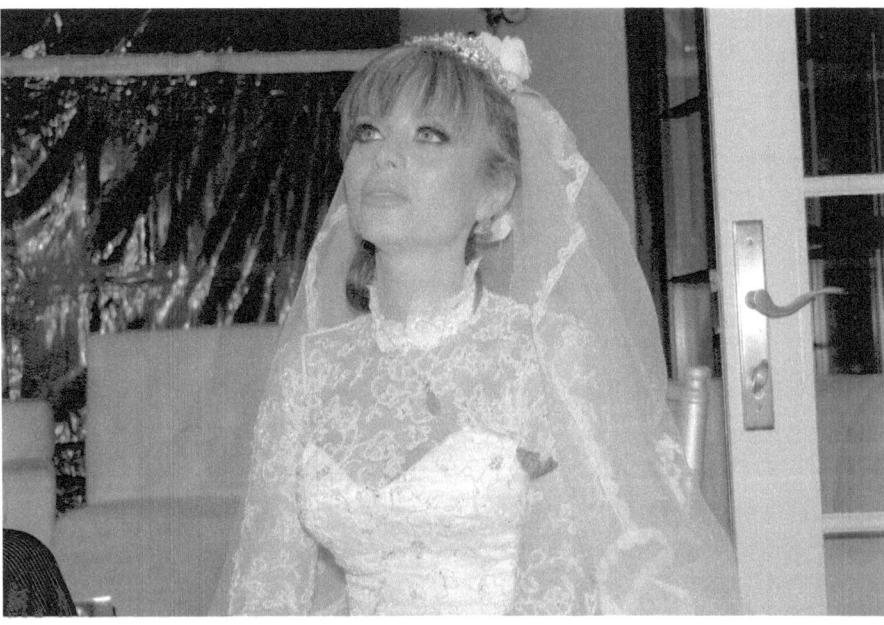

CHAPTER ONE

The Basics

What Kind Of Camera Should You Use?

Chances are good that you already have a camera of some kind, maybe several of them, and if that is the case be sure to read the rest of this book before you invest in a more expensive camera. The camera you have may be very good and can take better pictures if you apply a few simple rules. It's quite possible to spend thousands of dollars on the best camera that's available and use it to take shots that are still in the realms of just average, but you are striving for much better than just average and may be able to get by quite nicely with what you have or something you can get for a few hundred dollars or even less. Then again it could be that you have enjoyed the camera you have, got a lot of use from it, enjoyed it immensely but would like to move on to the exciting adventure of using something more advanced.

If you are ready to move on to the next level, really don't like the camera you have or have not got one yet, there are many very good cameras to choose from that will do quite a good job for you. Many people use small inexpensive pocket cameras that have very good picture quality with a high pixel count, which is the important thing. Pixels are the number of dots per inch that are on the photograph. The more dots per inch used to make the picture the better the quality. You should probably use a camera that has a rating of at least 8 mega-pixels, but if you have a camera that is only rated at 5 mega-pixels you may be able to get by with it, depending upon for what purpose your shots are going to be used. If you apply the basic principles you will be taking good photos.

The camera I have used for several years for professional photography did not cost thousands of dollars, but only about $800 and is now available in a newer model for a few hundred less. It's an 8 mega-pixel model by Canon known as the Rebel XT. The model that replaced it is a Rebel XT-i. I also use a Canon XH-A1 high definition camcorder for recording movies, which costs about $4,000. But if you also want to record movies you may be able to find something much less that will do a very nice job for you. In fact many of the small pocket still cameras can also take high definition movies by taking a lot of photos very rapidly, and have excellent quality. The difference is that some smaller cameras that may also be used to take movies may not have as much memory capability as you might like, which can result in a shorter movie. You will have to look at the specifications and features on the cameras in order to decide which one will be best for your purposes.

Here is an example of one of the inexpensive but excellent pocket cameras. A friend of mine recently put a home video online that completely amazed me with the quality that I was seeing. It was a short several minute video of her trip to Disneyland that had such good quality I was compelled to watch it several times. I was surprised to find that it was taken with one of those small pocket cameras that also allows for very high quality movies with excellent sound. Of course I had to know what kind of camera she had used and was surprised to find the cost of her Fuji Film J20 to be less than $200.00. My friend's pocket camera cost much less than my camera I use for professional photos and has a ten mega-pixel rating. This is just one example of many of the excellent small pocket cameras that are on the market, with more and better models becoming available all the time.

Since the small pocket cameras are so good then why would anyone want to spend so much more on one of the expensive cameras? The fact is no one would want to spend more, unless they wanted the extra advantages that some of the more expensive cameras offer, such as more setting selections that provide a wider range of flexibility for various kinds of shots. A more expensive camera may also allow for more memory for taking a larger number of shots, or a longer movie, before having to put in another memory card. There are many differences that are important to consider when shopping for your camera. We have to ask ourselves if we are going to be using the camera for professional, semi-professional or hobby use. If for mostly a hobby many of the pocket cameras would work out nicely. If for semi or professional use we would probably like one of the more expensive models.

In comparing my Canon Rebel XT with my friend's Fuji Film J20 I can get quite envious with some of the shots I've seen her take, but I have to remember that my friend uses her camera exclusively for photos of her, her friends and family, and does not do professional photography. Yet it would seem that there could be some professional applications with her less expensive model. When we take a closer look we see that I have more flexibility with my camera that allows me to use any of the special interchangeable lenses that are available from the manufacturer. For example, in addition to photographing actors and models, I also have done a lot of photographing and filming of airplanes, which requires a telephoto lens in order for me to get the best shots.

Four Basic Steps For Good Shots

The four primary things you need to remember when taking a good photo are

1 - The lighting,
2 - Get close enough to the subject,

3- Keep distracting obstructions out of the shot and

4 - Take a good number of shots of the same scene or subject to ensure you have several good ones from which to choose as your final selection.

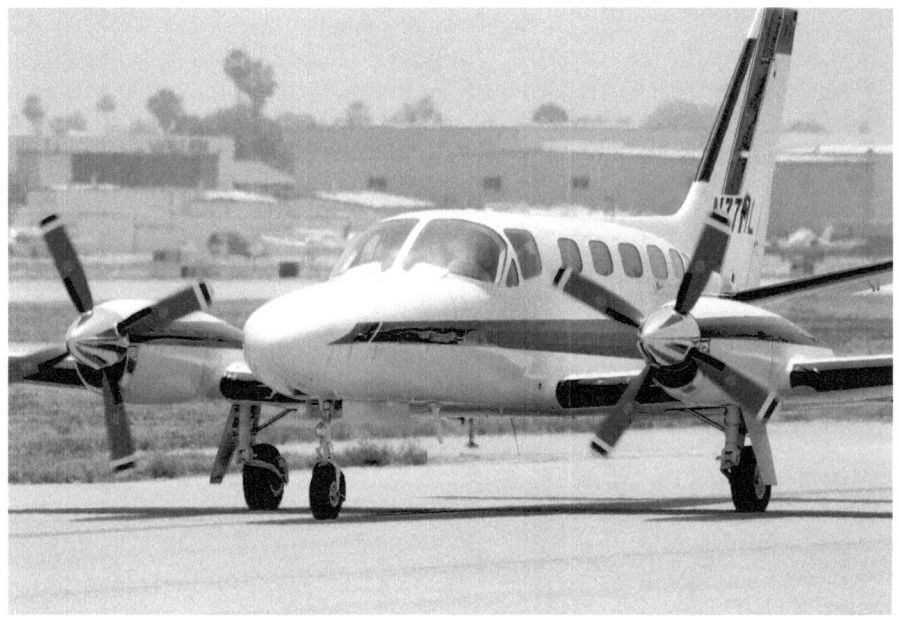

Lighting

It's an interesting thing about cameras and photos. The cameras need light in order to create good photos. And of course the best light is outdoors on a sunny day. We can get by on a cloudy day and do some touch up on the computer if it's really cloudy. But even on a sunny day you might be surprised at the difference you get when you use a flash. Why would you want to use a flash when you have all that sunlight? Try a few with a flash on a sunny day and you will see quite a difference. You will notice that with the flash you can easily eliminate unwanted shadow on the side of a person's face, if you get a shot where your subjects face is not entirely lighted by the sun.

You want to avoid shooting against the sun, but it can easily happen if you have a person or persons you are photographing and they happen to be walking around and end up with their back to the sun. It's a normal inclination for someone who is having their picture taken to turn their back to the sun. And your subject often will not be thinking of the fact that they should not have their back to the sun, and it can happen that you get a shot that you like but their back is against the sun. If it happens that you take that shot against the sun a flash can mean the difference between a good shot without the shadow, or a bad shot that you will not be able to use.

Again, it's a normal and almost an automatic thing for your subject or subjects to turn away from the sun to keep it out of their eyes, and it may be necessary to having their back toward the sun to get any kind of a shot at all, but this can be a detriment to your getting the best shots when it happens.

For ideal conditions it's good to schedule your photo shoot around mid-day when the sun will be higher in the sky and less in the eyes of your subject(s). The example shots below are some that were taken when the sun was about in the noon or 1:00pm position. The position of the sun and the superb job the camera made it difficult to make any real improvements on some of these near perfect shots. But there were some with face shadow could be removed by brightening the photo.

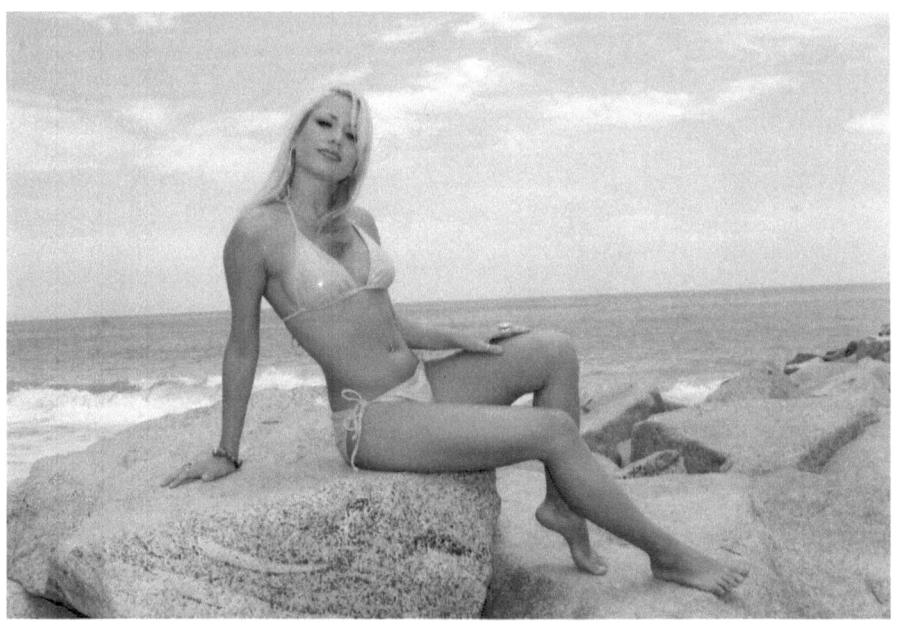

Raw Photo – No Re-Touching

Notice that the two photos on the next page are actually the same photo, but the first is darker than the second. Unlike many of the photos that were taken this day the timing on the camera or flash did not do quite the perfect job that it did with others, making the shot come out darker. With a little help from our editing software we can make an improvement, as seen in the second of the two photos that has been re-touched.

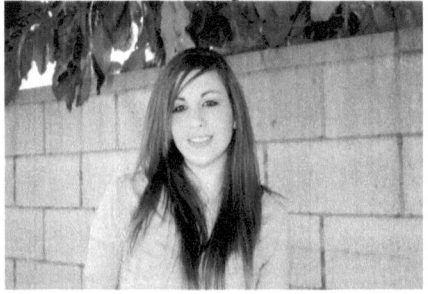
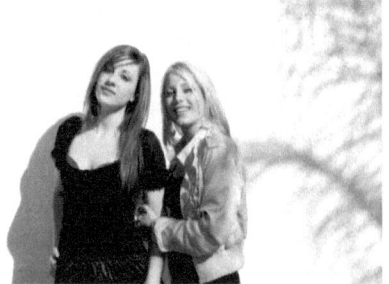

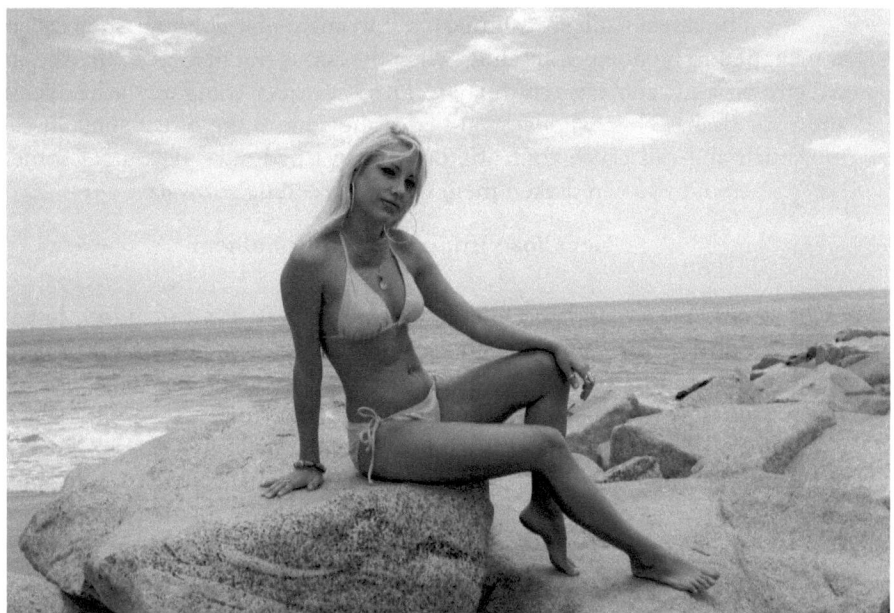

Raw – Not Re-Touched

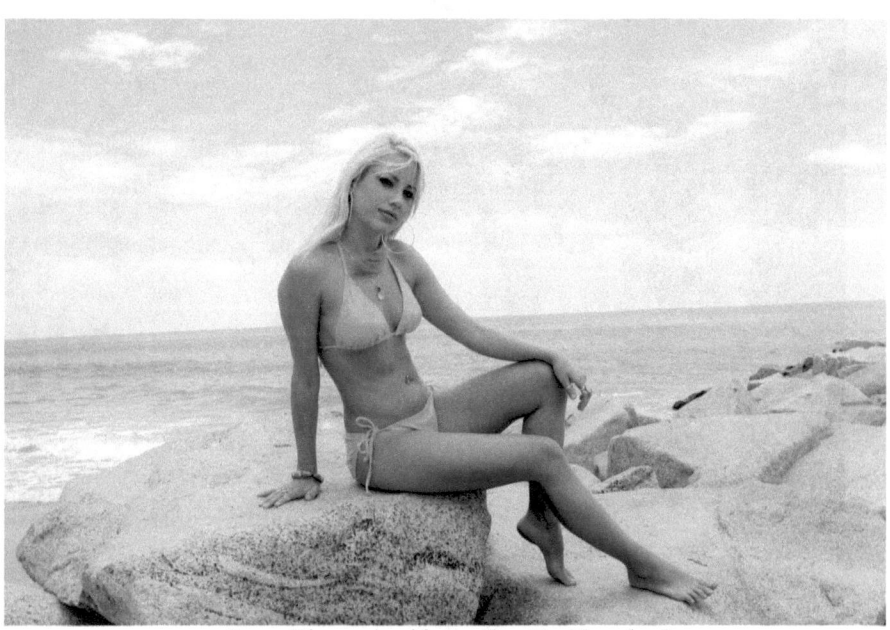

Same Photo As Above But Re-Touched

The second photo above was re-touched using the Smart Photo Fix feature of Corel Paint Shop Pro. The brightness and shadow settings were adjusted to make this improvement.

The direct sunlight can make it uncomfortable for your subjects, and if you happen to be doing your shots when the sun is not highest in the sky, and is directly on your subjects, you may want to consider using any available shade and your flash. This will give you better shots since the direct sunlight can be too much and can cause your photos to be washed out. If you get some that are washed out you can darken them with your editing software.

Get Close Enough To Your Subject

This may sound too simple and obvious to even mention, but if we think about it we have all seen shots where the subject is simply too far away from the camera. If you're using an inexpensive camera that does not have a zoom then you will just have to get closer to the subject to really get a good shot. If we are trying for a particular artistic effect by having the subject way off in the background then that is different and completely acceptable. But in looking at a lot of photos people take we often notice that what is an obscure shot of a subject could have been a fabulous photo if the person taking the shot had only got closer to the subject. If your lens will zoom even just a little it can mean the difference of a good shot or a bad one.

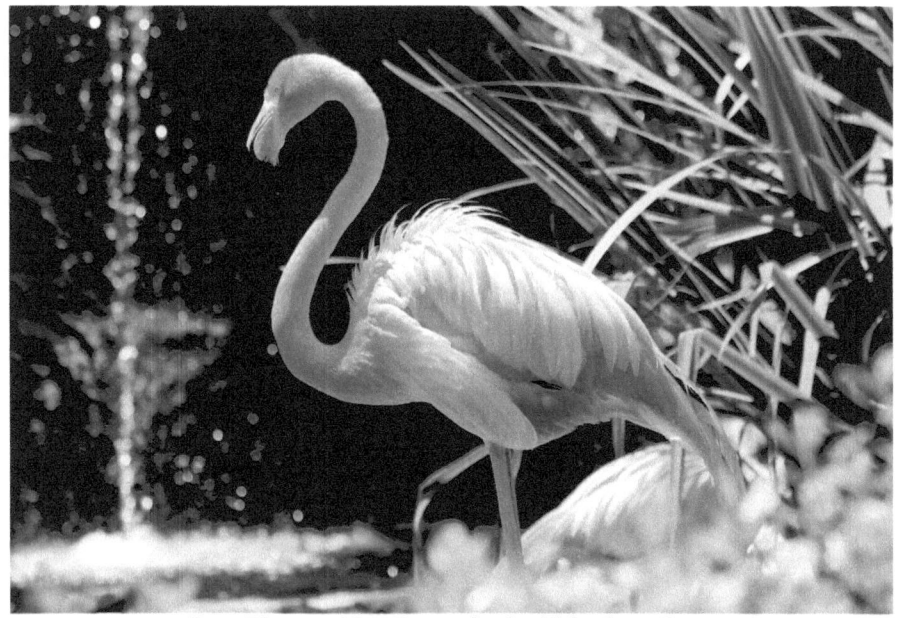

Raw Photo – Not Retouched – Telephoto Lens

Keep Distractions Out Of Your Shot

This can and does sometimes take a little more effort to accomplish, but the end result is well worth it. What do we mean by distractions or obstructions? For example, let's say we have a photo as seen below on the left.

At first glance we may not notice anything wrong with the shot, but when we take a closer look at it we find that there are things behind the subjects that don't really need to be there, and the shot will look better if those unnecessary things are not in the picture, as seen in the second and similar photo.

The boat behind the people in the first shot is a distraction and detracts from the quality of the photo. The boat can be edited out but that's a lot of work, easier to take the shot or another shot without the boat behind the people. The second photo on the right also has a boat behind the people but it is not a distraction because of its position, and actually compliments and is descriptive to the photo.

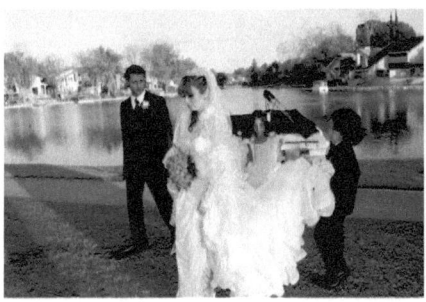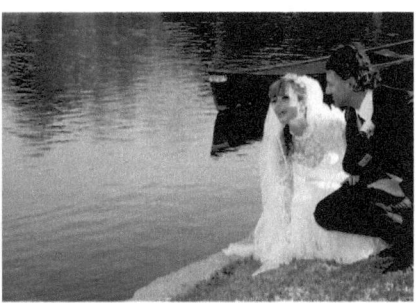

We want to avoid shots where objects are to the rear or side of our subjects if we can see they will be a distraction by creating a problem. If something is partially or fully showing to the side or rear of the subjects it makes the shot look messy and cluttered. This can lead to people using the expression, "she has a picture growing out the side of her head," when the photo hanging on the wall behind her is a part of the shot. It's better to pick another background when taking the shot, or take the picture off the wall while we get the shot. In the case of the first photo above it's simply a matter of stepping to the right or left a few feet and take the shot where the boat in the background is gone.

Of course if we really like a particular shot very much except for the distraction, we can re-touch the shot and remove the obstruction with Photo Shop or Paint Shop Pro, but a good rule to use that will save a lot of photo editing and re-touching is to check the background prior to taking the shot and make adjustments accordingly. Re-touching is a wonderful option for us to be able to use but we don't want to make a career of it, and there are some things that really cannot be re-touched at all. This is an example of letting the camera do most the work for you.

Sometimes the solutions to a problem can be so obvious and so close to us that we don't even see it. Being a professional photographer who has taken many thousands of shots of people, anyone would think it would have been instantly clear to me, no pun intended, but when I was recently doing a self-portrait, something that is not at all my favorite thing to do, every one of the couple dozen shots came out blurry. It was the most stupid feeling, looking at the photos and seeing my face was blurry and all the many distractions in the background were crystal clear. I had to laugh at myself and decided to practice what I preach by moving away from the background with all the junk in it, such as my computer screen, a desk lamp, sticky notes on the wall and on and on. When I simply turned my chair toward a wall that provided much fewer distractions I found my face to be crystal clear in all the photos, without the camera working so hard to blur me out and catch very clear shots of all my background junk.

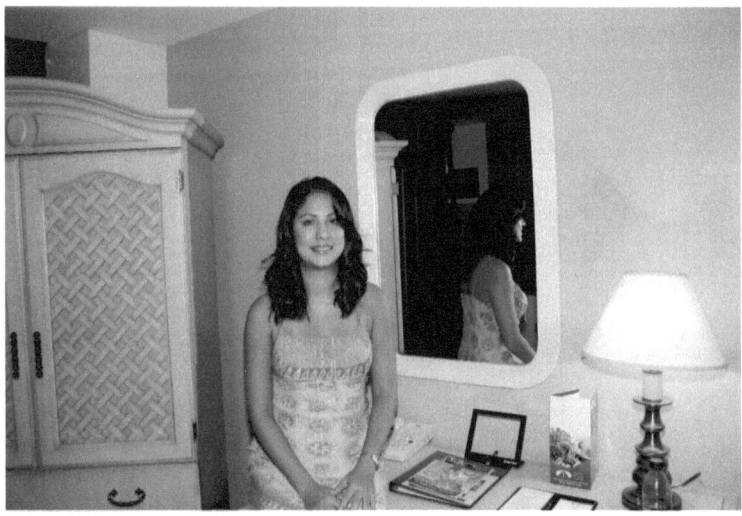

Here is another example of getting close enough and keeping distractions out. Nothing wrong with the photo above but we do notice a lot of things in the picture that we don't need, and if we want to get a better shot we can also move a little closer to the subject as we see in the shot below.

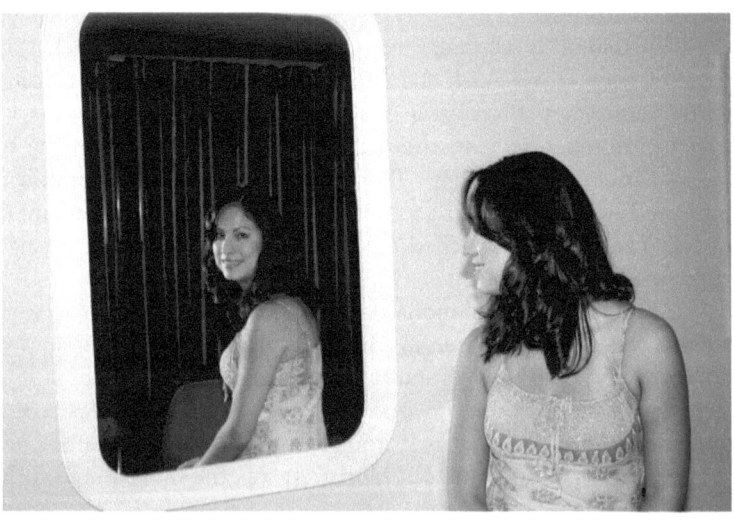

This photo is enhanced with the effect of using the mirror and is much nicer than the first without all the un-needed distractions, and if we want to go a step further and make another improvement we can also remove the chair showing in the background of the mirror.

Red Eye Removal

We've all seen photos of people that look like vampires or ware wolves because their eyes are red. This is caused by a technical phenomena that is very simple to understand if you are a rocket scientist, but who cares? All we know is that it is something we don't want. Red eye completely ruins what are otherwise many times very good photos. If you happen to get a shot and your subjects have red eye you can remove the red eye with your photo editing software, but that can be extra work. Your camera may have a setting for red eye prevention that will be easier to use and much less time consuming than editing the photos.

More Subtle Distractions

Make Sure Your Subjects Are Well Rested

Make Sure Your Subjects Are Not Hungry

Another type of distraction that we often times may not think about is the following. People's eyes and mouths have sometimes opened with surprise when I have asked them to make sure they are well rested before their photo shoot, but it does make a difference. We don't want our photos of people looking like police mug shots. If someone complains about photos you have taken of them you may want to ask yourself, "how well rested was the subject?" Did your subject get a good nights rest? If your subject did not get enough rest it may very likely show in their photos. If your subject has red eyes maybe they were out late and were maybe drinking and are tired. If this is the case you may want to postpone taking the photos until another time when your subject(s) has had more rest, looks and feels better, if possible. How people feel does affect how they look.

Otherwise, if you find yourself having to take the shots of someone or a number of people who are tired, you may find yourself doing a great deal of re-touching in order for the photos to be at all acceptable.

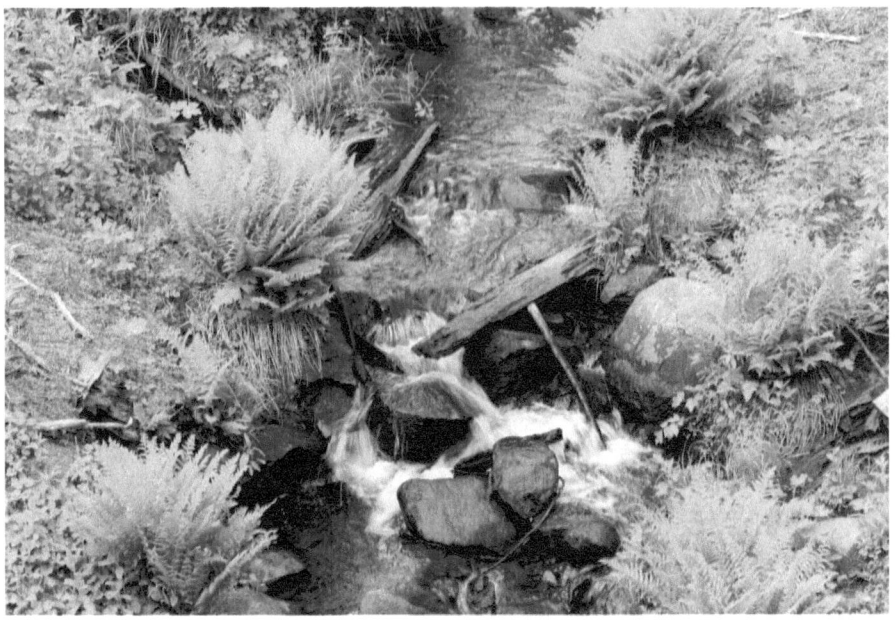

It's perhaps not as serious a thing as lack of sleep, but if a person is hungry and has not eaten recently it can and does affect the way they feel, and in turn also affects how they appear in their photos. If someone is hungry their metabolism is down which does have an effect, however slight it may be, on their appearance. You always want your subject to be at their best, to look their best and to feel their best as well, and someone who has not eaten for a while may not at all be at their best in the way they feel and look. So what are you going to do, carry around a bunch of Happy Meals for people who never eat? Yes, if you have to, and want to get the best shots, or at least tell them the day before to make sure they eat good.

Of course we can and sometimes do have to work around such things as the person is tired, hungry or even in a bad mood, but making sure someone is well rested, not hungry and in good spirits can bring us closer to the ideal conditions were looking for to get our near perfect shots. Taking photos of people when they have just experienced any kind of misfortune in life is not the time to take their photos. It's best to pick another happier time.

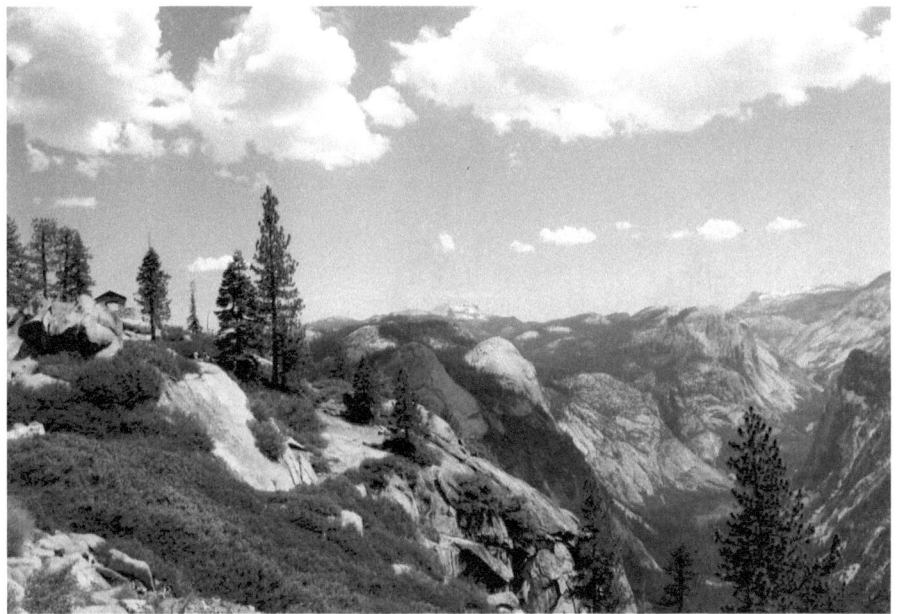

Take A Good Number Of Shots Of The Same Scene

Why take so many? Some people have asked me this while making a face at me when getting so annoyed with so much flash from the camera. We need to take a lot because it's better to be safe than sorry.

No matter how hard we try it can be difficult, if not impossible to get that great shot by taking only one. This is why we see the professionals taking so many, often to the dismay of the subjects with the flash going off so much, but getting a lot of shots increases our chances of getting that perfect one that we are looking for. In taking several photos of a small group of people at a wedding party I was disappointed that I wouldn't be able to use any of the four photos. Everything seemed perfect. The background, people and lighting were all fine. Everything was good. It was a group of four people and in each photo a different one of the people managed had their eyes closed. If I had persisted and taken just a few more shots of the group chances would be good that I could have gotten one or two very good shots with everybody's eyes open. Some days it just doesn't pay to get out of bed (unless we take a few extra shots)!

It can take a little persistence and persuasion when photographing a person or group, to get them to hold still while you snap a dozen or so shots. Many people are under the impression that two or three shots will be enough, but you will find that if you are fortunate enough to have a fast camera you will do much better by taking at least a dozen shots or so of the same scene. If someone doesn't blink, your flash timing wasn't just right, it's always something that can and does go wrong with just one or two shots, which can be remedied simply by just taking a lot of shots of the same scene.

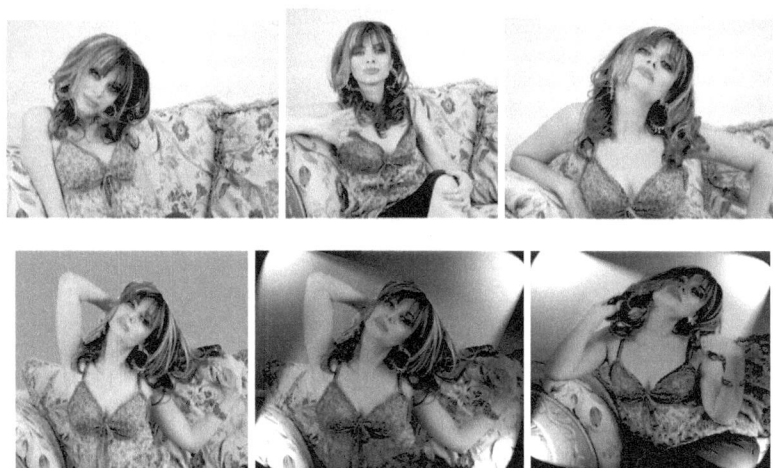

Some Special Lighting Effect Applied With Photo Editing Software

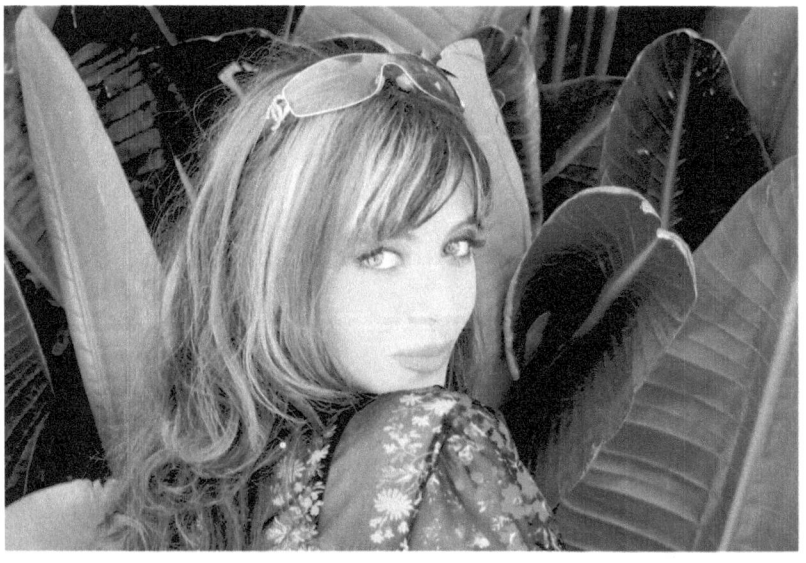

CHAPTER TWO

Shooting Indoors

Photography indoors can almost be described as an entirely different world. But with a little help it doesn't have to be as difficult as it can be. We just have to pay attention again to the lighting, which is different because we don't have the sun helping us. We are even more dependent upon the flash and can sometimes even use some extra lighting in addition to the flash to ensure our shots come out very nice.

Consider Indirect Lighting

With indoor lighting we can simply use the flash on our camera, or we can use some additional lighting in order to get the best shots possible. Floodlights can be used if the situation permits. But whether using floodlights and a flash or just the flash we want to keep in mind that direct lighting is not always the best. In other words it can be better to bounce the flash or floodlighting off a ceiling or wall in order to really get the very best shots. It can make a big difference in providing a softer lighting source that does not wash out the subject. A little rehearsal or experimentation if there is time to do it can be very good in helping us determine if the direct or indirect lighting will be best.

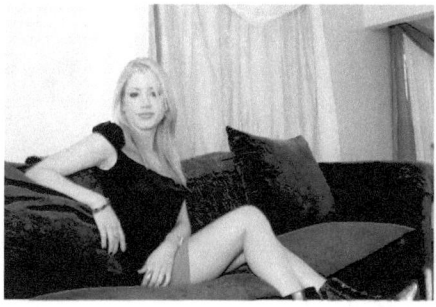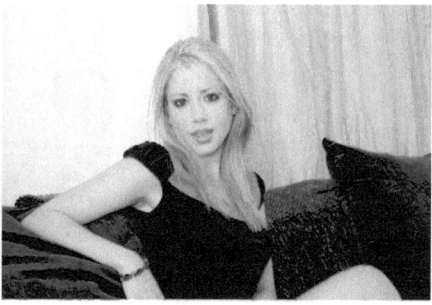

Both shots are okay but the one on the right is better. We can even go a step further to improve this shot by taking it again without the curtain behind the girl.

If the room lighting is very dim it can be quite difficult to get a good shot even using the flash. With some cameras you need a minimum amount of light for the camera to be able to focus. With SLRs (Single Lens Reflex) for example, such as the camera I use, the lens focuses on the subject when you press the button half way. But if there is not enough light for the lens to focus when you squeeze the button your shot can come out blurry and out of focus.

When taking photos at a party it can be socially awkward when trying to get some good shots. At parties you want to be polite and not be too much of a distraction to guests with your flash. And make sure you do not become the center of attention by staying to the rear an out of the way as much as possible. But particularly if someone requests a certain shot of some kind, and the lights are very low we may just have to ask if it will be okay to turn some lights on in the room while we get a few shots.

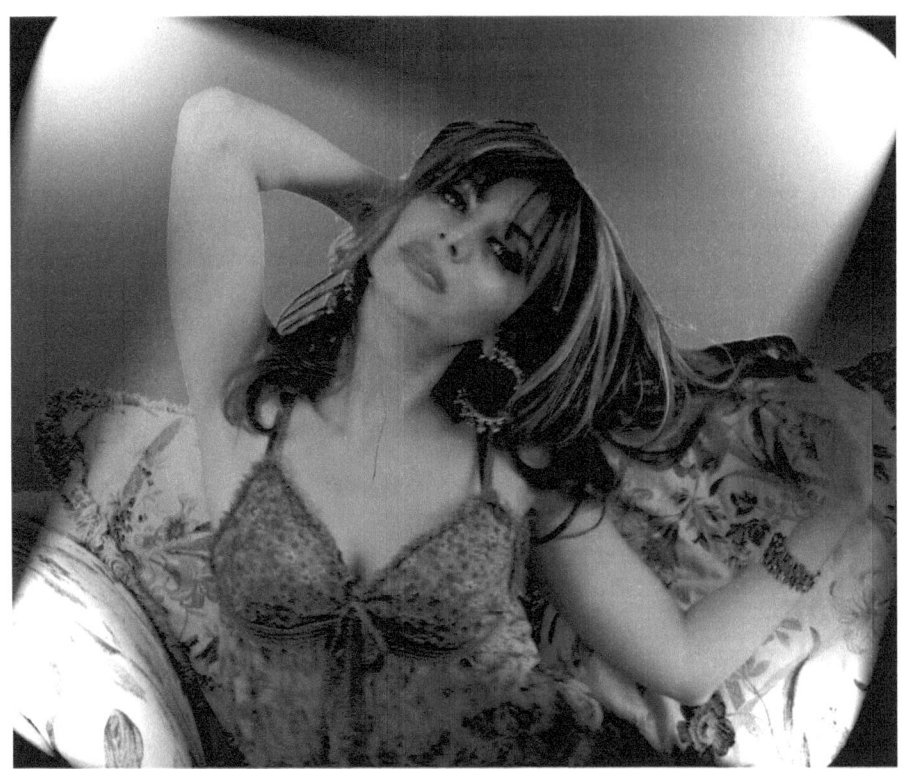

Using Special Lighting Effects With Our Editing Software

Night Photography

Taking pictures at night can be a lot of fun and a bit more challenging as well compared to daytime shots with the help of the sun. Since there isn't as much light for the camera to work with the night shots will be darker and the camera has to work harder to keep the shots from being blurry. It's best to use the night setting on our cameras if we have them. Using the night settings makes the lens of the camera stay open longer to get the shot with a slower shutter speed.

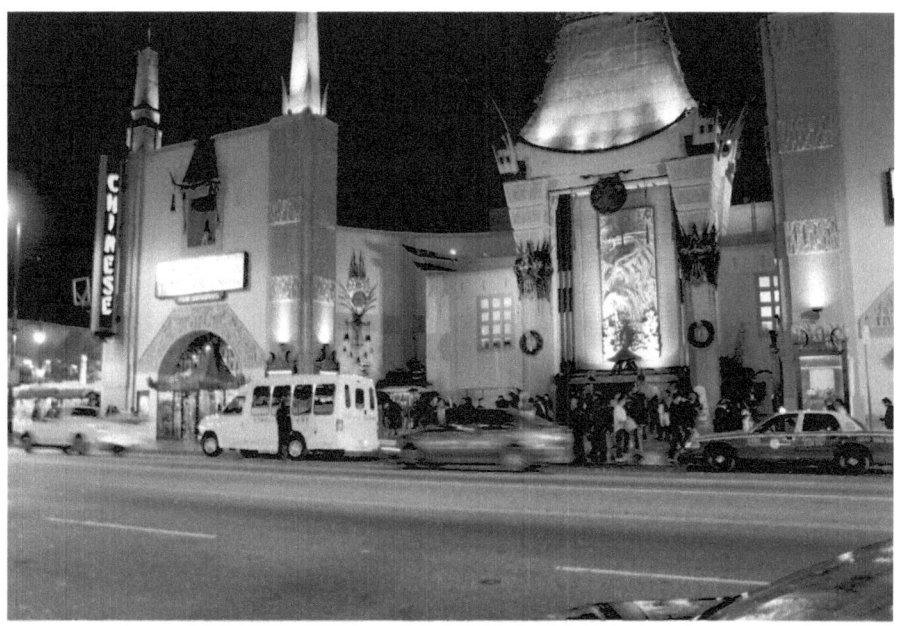

When using a smaller amount of light, maybe coming from only streetlights, buildings, signs and so forth the longer the lens of the camera will have to stay open to get the shot. It can take a little or maybe even a lot of practice to get some good night shots until we learn the winning combination of settings on our camera. Your camera may have just one setting for night photos. If it has more settings it's good to learn about them and experiment a little to find which settings work best.

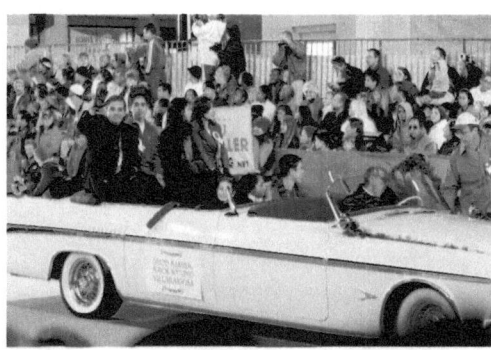

This is actually a night shot also but there is enough light from the parade activities to get a pretty good shot from a distance of about 100 feet.

23

Should You Use A Tripod?

As to whether or not you should use a tripod depends upon the situation and the type of camera you are using. One of the primary uses of tripods has always been to avoid camera movement that would blur a shot. A tripod can be helpful in preventing blurry shots even with most modern cameras, but will likely not be needed as much as with older cameras. Many of the more modern cameras have an image stabilization feature that is very helpful in eliminating the blurry shots. A tripod might be suggestible if using an older film camera or older movie camera that do not have the built-in image stabilization feature. Even if your camcorder has image stabilization using a tripod can be most helpful if you are taking video with a very powerful zoom lens. The powerful zoom can make it difficult to keep your image steady without the tripod even with your built-in image stabilization.

Tripods can be useful even with the more modern cameras particularly if you want to mount it in a spot and shoot from a distance from the camera with a remote control device. Another use would be in a situation where you are at the photo location for a long time and might get tired of holding the camera, such as an airfield or outdoors spot taking photos of wildlife. But the downside to a tripod is that it limits the control to some degree as to how fast you can move the lens into position when you see that special shot you want to get. For example, if your camera is mounted on a tripod and you notice something behind you and want to get the shot, it is much more difficult to quickly turn to your rear and get the shot with your camera on the tripod.

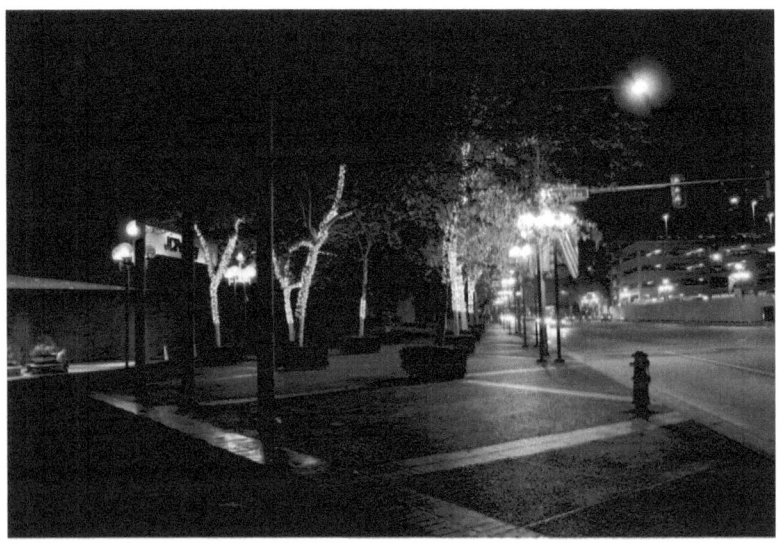

A tripod can be very nice if you are at or having a party, for example, and you would like to take some video or still shots remotely with you in the scene. You can mount your camera on the tripod and set your camera to take timed shots a few seconds after you press the button and step into the scene, or use a remote device to press the shutter button. Or with your video camera or camcorder you can start it running, step into the scene and let the video run as long as you want. You may have to do quite a bit of editing depending upon how professional you want the results to be.

Another use for a tripod is night shots that can require the camera be as still as possible with not as much light to work with at the slower shutter speeds.

If we are not using a flash and are dependent upon the light from streetlights, buildings etc., we find the shutter speed on the camera is slower, with the camera taking longer to get the shot with less light to work with.

You may have heard of time-lapse photography. If you haven't heard of it you have probably seen it, maybe without knowing how it's done. It can be a fun way of doing night photography. This is when a camera is set to take a photo very slowly and can have some interesting and artistic effects. Time-lapse videos can be created as well by setting the camera to take a single frame every few seconds rather than running continually. When played back we might see a storm coming in with the clouds moving very quickly, as an example.

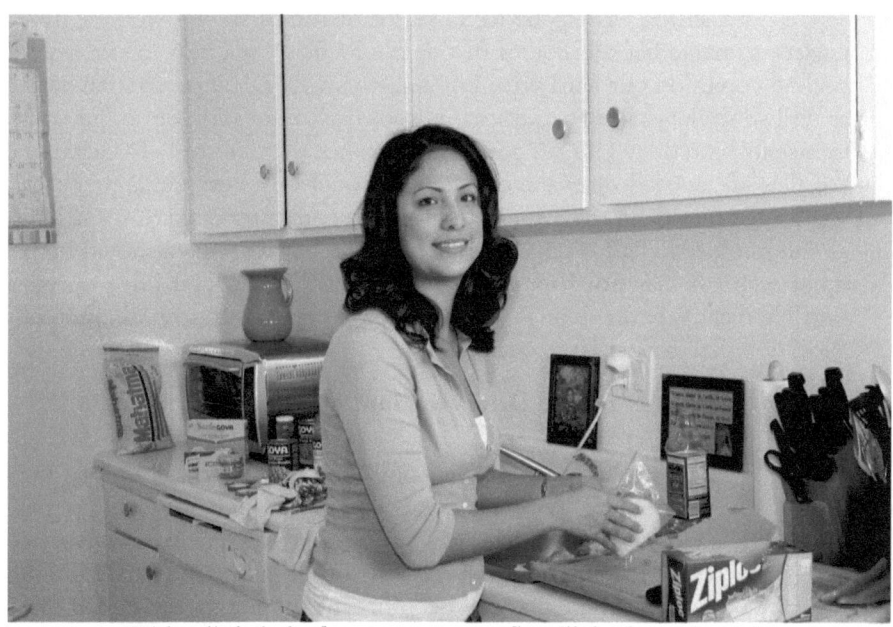

With a little help from some extra floodlight from the right

CHAPTER THREE

Tips For Working With Your Photo Files

A few good things to remember when working with our photos on the computer after we have taken our shots are, make backup copies, rename files you have touched up an and some advantages to an external disc and hard drives.

As amazing as our computers are with the many tasks they help us perform it's important for us to remember that our computers are not perfect, and they can and do sometimes cause errors.

Be Sure To Backup Files

It's all too easy to be having a lot of fun as we are working away and neglect to make backup copies of our photo files. It's best to not only make backup copies on our hard drive but also on a CD, DVD or external hard drive as well so we have a copy of everything somewhere in addition to our computer in case its hard drive fails. A good idea is to make a CD or DVD backup before the files are deleted from the camera. It would be a very unhappy occasion if we deleted files from the camera and found a computer error of some kind, and all the photos we had taken are gone. Any of our work files should be backed up as well. It may not happen often but when a computer error occurs it's a horrible feeling, particularly if we do not have copies of our work, preferably in a location that is external to our computer.

External Disc Drives & Hard Drives - Advantages

You may have heard people complain about it taking so long for their photos to load from a CD or DVD. If you are using high quality photo files they are likely quite large in size, which take a lot of system resources to load and view. Slow loading and viewing can be because of a small amount of memory on your machine that can be improved by putting more memory on it. But you may find that an external CD or DVD drive will make things faster also. An external hard drive or disc drive can run you a few hundred dollars, but if you work a lot with the large photo files you might find the cost well worth it. In addition to improved performance with an external CD or DVD drive, you will get a longer life from the CD/DVD drive that came with your machine. The drives that come with our machines are often not as rugged or heavy duty as the external drives that can also be used for copying discs.

Renaming Touched Up Files

After re-touching a photo change the file name when you save it so you have the original to work with later if you need it for any reason. For example if you select file Img001 to modify, make your modifications, then when you save the changed file change the file name from Img_001 to Img_001R. This will save you the frustration of not being able to start from the beginning with the original file, if you decide at some time later that you would like to make a different modification of the original file.

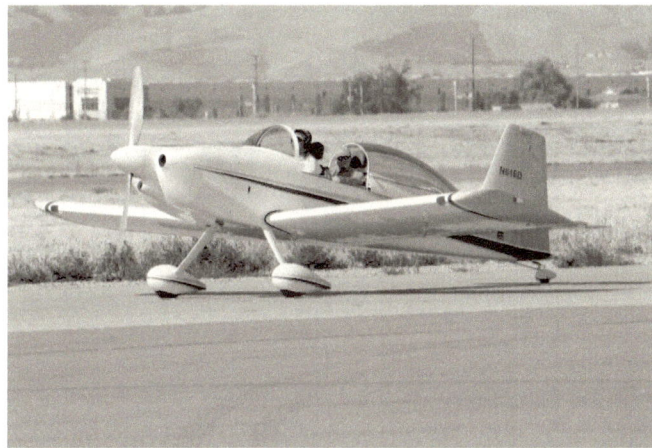
Img_077

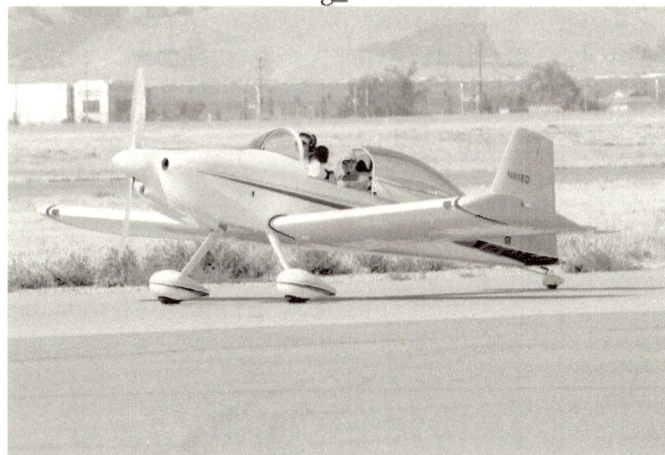
Img_077R

Tips For Equipment Care

Photography Widows

It's not like you really think of your camera as if it were your child, but when you wake up and see your wife standing there with that look that tells you she is a little concerned with the camera you have lying next to you while you were sleeping, maybe it's a good idea to spend a little more time with her for a while. You don't want her to feel too much like a photo widow.

Care of your camera(s) is mostly a matter of basic common sense. Just don't do anything to any of your cameras or other electronic equipment such as cell phones, that you wouldn't want done to yourself. Extreme temperatures, high or low are not good. Cameras and electronic devices do not mix well with moisture. You would not want to use your camera in sub-zero weather conditions without having it protected with a special covering of some kind. Nor would you want to take it in a sauna with you at a temperature of 185 degrees, even if it's a dry heat sauna.

No Swimming

If you drop a cell phone in water, or spill a liquid on a computer keyboard do not expect them to work again. The same is true with your camera. If you are on a small boat on a lake or the ocean with some pretty good size waves, no matter how tempting it might be to get a few extra shots or some extra footage, if that water is coming up near you and your camera, you had better put the camera in the case and put it below to keep it dry.

Even on a very humid day it may be too much for your camera. Your pocket flash camera might make it, but your camcorder may not do so well since it has more moving parts that are affected by the moisture. If it's humid enough some of the better camcorders automatically will shut down to prevent damage to its parts. There are cameras that fit into the category of special equipment that will work fine underwater, but most do not.

No Smoking

You wouldn't expect to be very healthy if you smoked a couple packs of cigarettes per day. Don't expect your photographic equipment, especially a camcorder to work well in smoky conditions.

You may want to think twice about using your expensive movie camera to take footage at a party where there is a smoke generating machine for special party effects. At a very minimum you can expect the thick and heavy party smoke to keep your camera from getting a good video, and the smoke could also do permanent damage to your camera. The same would be true in a fire condition with a lot of smoke. As tempting as it might be to get real close and get some exciting footage of the fire that the guys are trying to put out, do not do so if it means you will be putting yourself and your equipment at risk.

No Radiation

Best to keep all your electronic equipment turned off if you are quite close to active powerful radio transmitting equipment, like the radio in a small aircraft. Powerful radio beams can cause havoc with your digital equipment that uses electronic devices. Your electronic cameras can be damaged if not properly shielded and protected from powerful radio beams. See Chapter Seven for more detailed information on this.

CD/DVD Drives

Many of us put copies of our photos and movies on CDs or DVDs for storage or to share with our friends. It probably won't hurt anything if you leave a disc in the drive all the time, but it's best to take it out when not using it. When not using the CD/DVD drive in your computer it's best to remove the disc so the computer does not continually try to access the data on the disc, which some computers do. With some computers the processor and/or hard drive will tend to run continually when the CD or DVD is in the drive and not being used. When you start the computer it may look at the contents on the disc, which is unnecessary work for your computer, unless it's a start-up disc that you are using.

Batteries & Video Tapes

When not using your camera or camcorder it's best to remove your batteries and videotapes. Even if your camera is off there can be just a small amount of drain on the battery when it's in the camera. Tapes should not be stored in the camera and the manufacturers suggest keeping the tapes re-wound when being stored.

Tape Re-winder?

If you use your video camera a lot you might find it a good idea to invest in a tape re-winder. Using a tape re-winder rather than re-winding when the tape is in your camera can increase the length of your camera's tape-drive mechanism. Many good camcorders allow the user to do editing with the camera's tape drive, but your tape drive mechanism will last much longer if you do as much editing as you can with the software on your computer.

With the advancements we will see in coming years we can probably predict with some pretty good accuracy the end of the era of tapes. Cameras of the future will probably have enormous amount of flashcard type memory, making tapes obsolete. Some of the pocket cameras already can take movies with available memory. But for now, while some of us still use tapes, we want to get as much life from our tape-drive mechanism as possible, and a re-winder can help us do that.

Do You Have A Strap For That?

So, you are sixteen hundred feet above the ground taking some very nice video of the scenery. You are flying in that little helicopter with the door open on your side that is quite helpful for catching the view. The pilot looks at you with a frown and asks you on the intercom, "do you have a strap for that?" You nod your head and the pilot asks, "Well, where is it?" And without looking at the pilot you say, "in my car." You look at the ground sixteen hundred feet below, and wonder if the pilot is concerned mostly about the safety of your camera or who's head your camera might land on if it slips out of your hands. Personally, you are having so much fun you really don't care.

Your camera is a very delicate instrument, and unless it's a small pocket camera, if your camera has a strap that came with it, it's best to use the strap. Sure, you may look and feel silly with the camera or cameras hanging from your neck but it's much better to be safe than sorry. If the camera slips out of your hands you will be very glad if you are using the strap. The only time you should not use a strap is when you are at a party and near the pool. Take the strap off your neck when near the pool, because if you stumble and go into the pool, you don't want the camera coming in with you. You and your soggy clothing can survive the plunge but the camera cannot.

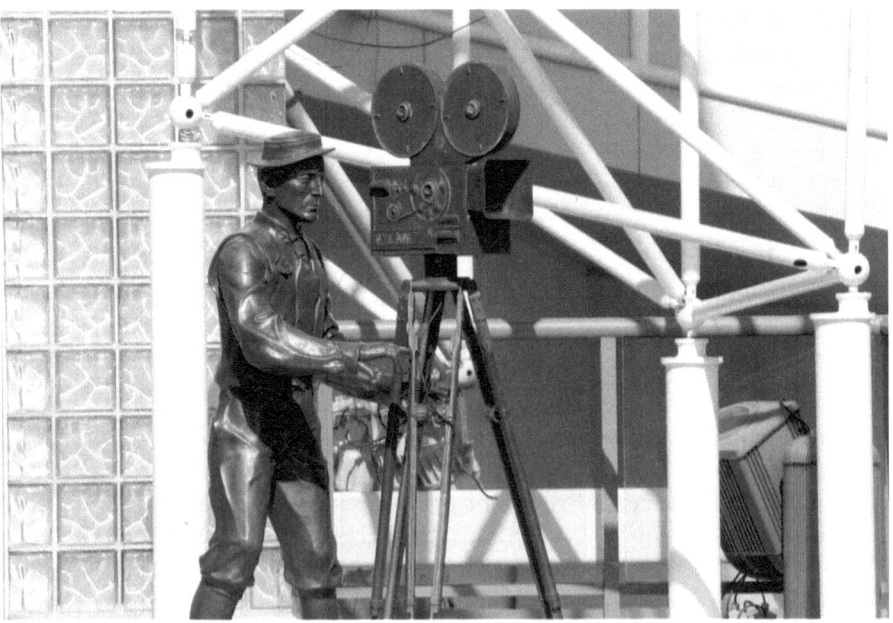

Chapter Four

Self Portraits

A lot of us like to take shots of ourselves to share with our friends on our social networking websites, and many of us take very good shots that can be improved by applying a few of the simple rules. Those rules are pretty much the same as for taking shots of others, and by applying these simple rules you will find your shots of yourself will be better and enjoyed more by your friends and family.

1 – The lighting,

2 - Get close enough to the subject,

3- Keep distracting obstructions out of the shot and,

4 – Take a good number of shots of the same scene or subject to ensure you have several good ones from which to choose as your final selection.

And of course to look your best don't forget the other sometimes overlooked rules of having enough rest and food before taking your self-portraits. Be sure not to take those photos of yourself after a long night of heavy partying, when you are ill with a cold or just really tired. Your images of yourself are important and will be how everyone sees you.

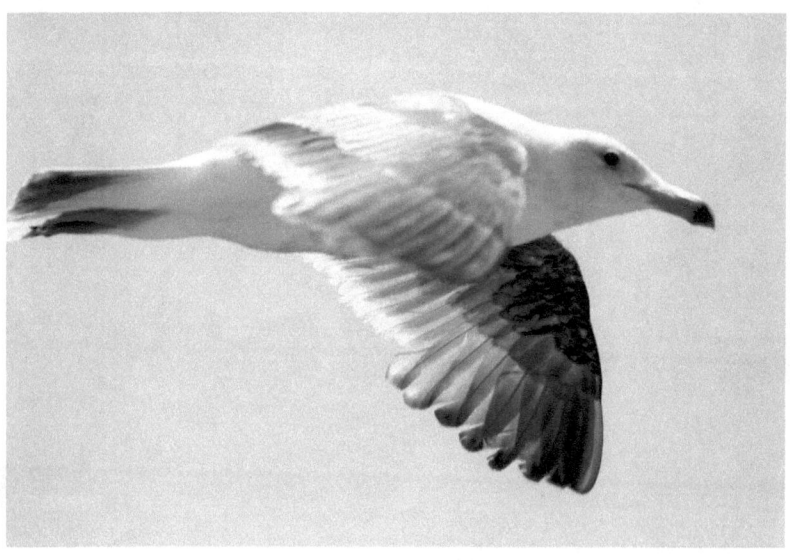

Re-Touching

Many people do not bother with re-touching at all. They take their photos and are maybe happy enough with the results that they really never think about making an improvement to any of their shots. Some of the cameras used do have amazing quality with no need in the case of many shots for touching up.

The cost of the software used to do the re-touching can but doesn't have to be high. It can be quite expensive particularly if you use Adobe Photo Shop that can cost as much as nearly $1,000.00. Of course Adobe is the premier and best you can get, used mostly for professional purposes, but you may be surprised with the outstanding results you can get from other photo editing software that will enable you to do many of the things you can do with Photo Shop. An example is Corel Paint Shop Pro that I have used for some years to re-touch professional photos, and the cost is only a fraction of that of Photo Shop. If you are a professional you may want to invest in Photo Shop to get the extra benefits it offers, but if you would like to keep your editing software within your budget Paint Shop Pro will do a very nice job for you.

If you like the idea of doing a minimum of photo editing or re-touching and don't really want to spend any money on software, there are a number of photo editing software programs that are available for free. Some of these free programs come with the purchase of the camera and can do a very nice job of helping you make improvements to many of your shots. If your camera did not come with free editing software this is not a problem. There are plenty of free photo editing programs readily available online at places such as Cnet's Download.com at http://download.Cnet.com/windows/

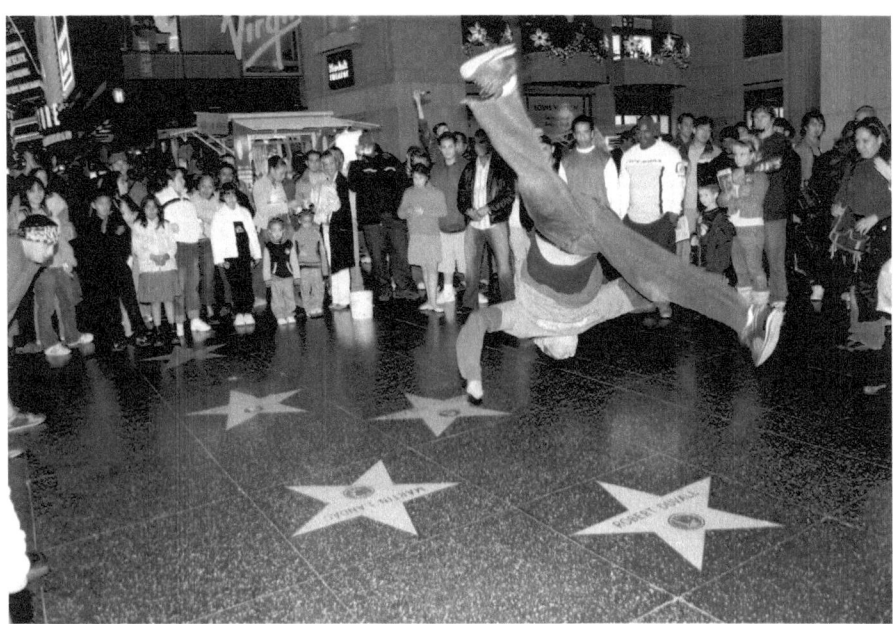

Let Your Camera Do Most The Work

As much fun as we might have in making improvements to our photos with editing software, there are only so many hours in a day, and we probably have other things we need to do as well. We can still have a good time touching up some of our favorite shots, while at the same time letting our camera do most of the work for us and keeping the re-touching to a minimum.

A good rule to follow is getting the best shots you can of your subject, which will reduce the amount of work you have to do in re-touching your photos. In fact it can save you tons of work if you are taking lots of photos, hundreds of them at a time. Letting the camera do most the work for you by using the correct setting, lighting and so forth is definitely the way to go.

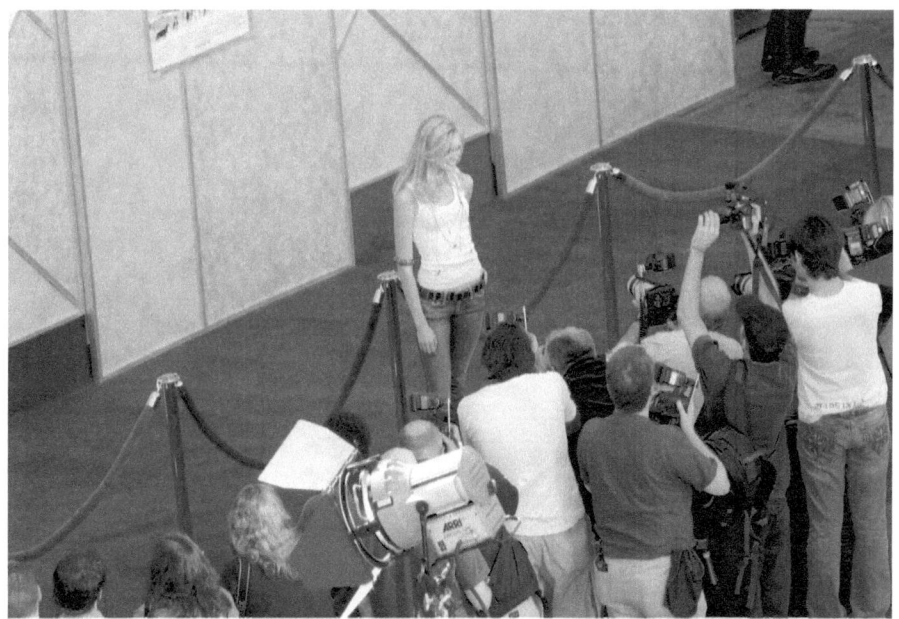

Not Too Bad A Shot Considering I Was 300 Yards Away

One of my most memorable experiences was doing a photo shoot with a model that was relatively new in this country. She was from Europe, had been photographed quite a lot and asked me before hand if I did the makeup and hair. I explained to her that I did not do the makeup and hair, and that she would have to do it herself or have someone help her with that. Since I didn't do hair or makeup she liked very much having her photos re-touched, so much so that she tended to rely on me, the photographer, to fix her lipstick, hair, makeup and so forth, after her photos had been taken. Nice work if you can get it.

As much as I appreciated getting the extra work, and wanting to accommodate her as much as possible, I explained to her that I would be happy to do a lot of extra re-touching when she neglected to fix her hair, makeup and lipstick the way she wanted them to be seen in her photos, but also explained that there would be a fee attached to all the extra work that I would be doing. When she got the bill for the photo shoot she started to do her hair, makeup and lipstick prior to the shots being taken. And when I showed her how to use software on her computer to do the re-touching herself, she was very happy with that.

Eventually the model from Europe and I became the best of friends, and I photographed her wedding party, weddings or wedding parties being something I don't normally do. I was glad to see that she and her new husband and all their family and friends did their hair, makeup and so forth, and were looking their best, which saved me a lot of touch-up work in preparing her wedding party album for her.

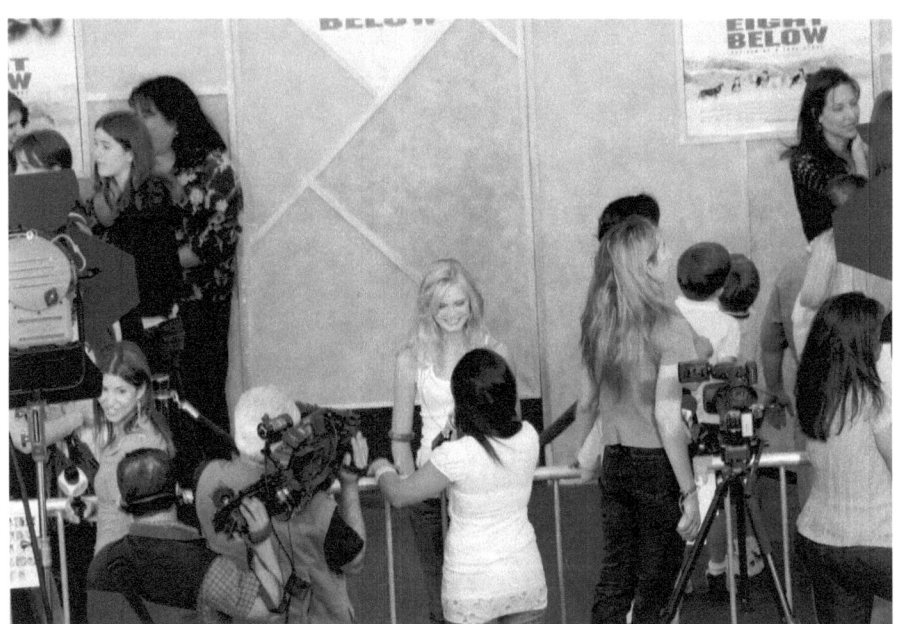

One Step Photo Fix

When using many of the cameras that are available it's nice to see that the camera has done such a nice job for us under the right conditions, that re-touching a photo may be completely unnecessary. But with many of the shots we take it's possible to get an improvement with our software. Paint Shop Pro has a button at the top that in many cases does a very nice One Step Photo Fix, that will brighten or darken the shot, whichever is needed and provide quite a good improvement.

Smart Photo Fix

The One Step Photo Fix can be used a number of times in order to get an improved photo, but on occasion we will find that it does not do the job exactly as we would like. In this case there is a button just below it labeled Smart Photo Fix that provides a very good interface for making a more detailed improvement with a number of different adjustments to our shot, such as brightness, shadow, saturation or color amount and so on. The Smart Photo Fix takes a few minutes longer than the One Step Photo Fix but is very useful in helping us make improvements.

We will notice in our photo editing software many other tools for making improvements, such as special effects and many other modifications to our photos, if we would like to use them. We can remove red-eye, blur the photo, make it a grayscale, negative, resize it and on and on. For the most part using the One Step Photo Fix or the Smart Photo Fix features are enough to get what we want, but it's nice to know that so many of the other tools are available if we have a need or desire for them.

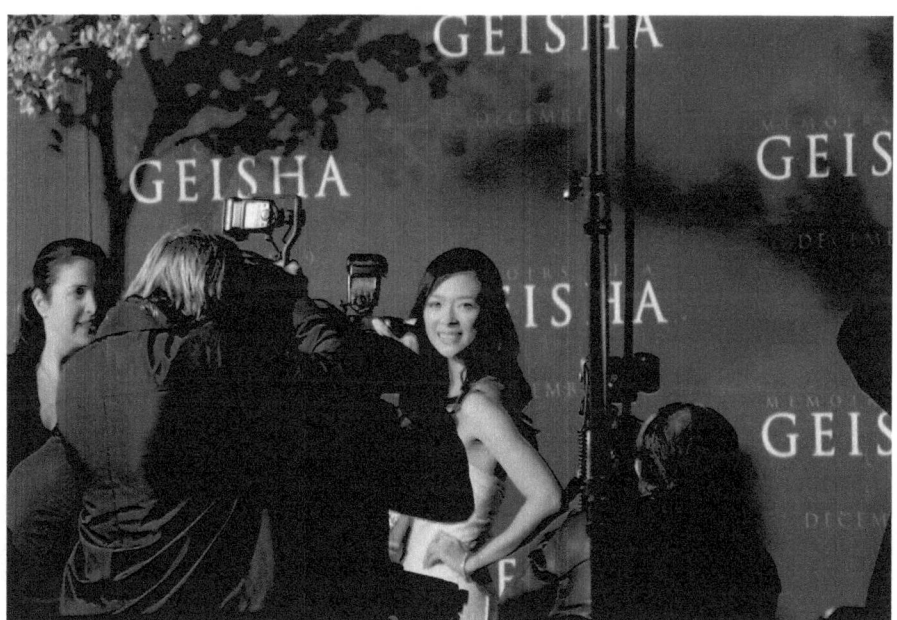

The Telephoto Lens Is Great For Use In Crowds

CHAPTER FIVE

Video Photography

Introduction

If there is anything more fun than taking a picture it is taking a motion picture. And if a picture is worth a thousand words, then a motion picture must be worth at least a million dollars. The first movie camera I ever saw was one my dad got when we were just little kids. It was a Bell & Howell 8mm with no sound but it was a very exciting adventure for the family when Dad would take movies of us, send the film off for processing and then be able to watch ourselves in the movie a few weeks later. The projector made a lot of noise just like you used to be able to hear in the movie theaters if you were close enough to the projection booth.

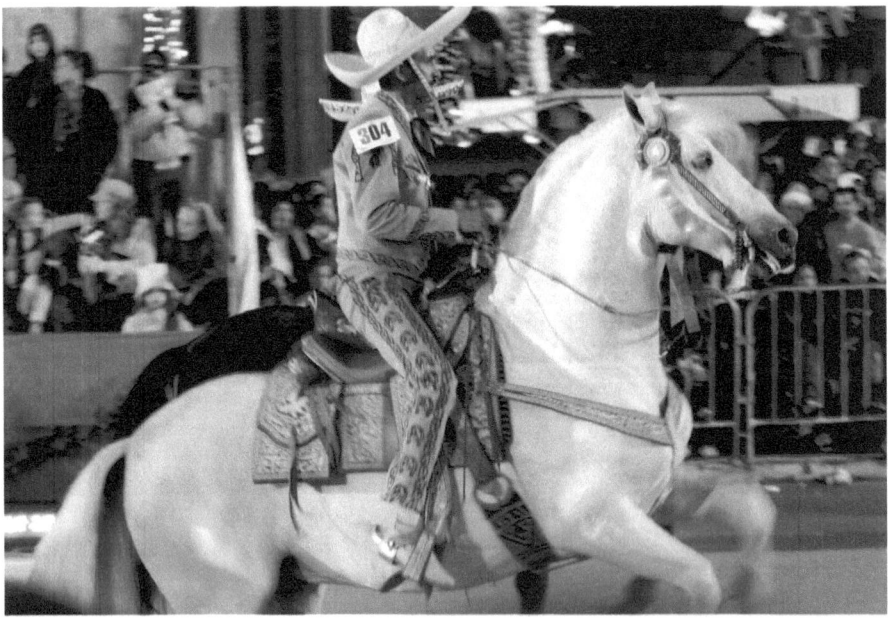

Although I've been taking photographs nearly all my life I didn't get my first movie camera or camcorder until about twenty years ago. Then I realized how much fun I had been missing. It was an inexpensive Canon camcorder that I bought new for a few hundred dollars, and I used it and enjoyed it so much that I actually wore it out in a couple years. Then I got a little more serious with a Canon GL-2 and found it to be my favorite thing of all time. With interchangeable lenses, some that were telephoto with as much as 100-power zoom, it would also take stills, although somewhat lower quality at only 1.2 mega-pixels, as well as excellent quality standard definition motion pictures using the DVD mini tapes. It had a number of special effects that were a lot of fun to use, such as scene transitions and so forth that can also be found in most of the video editing software that is available.

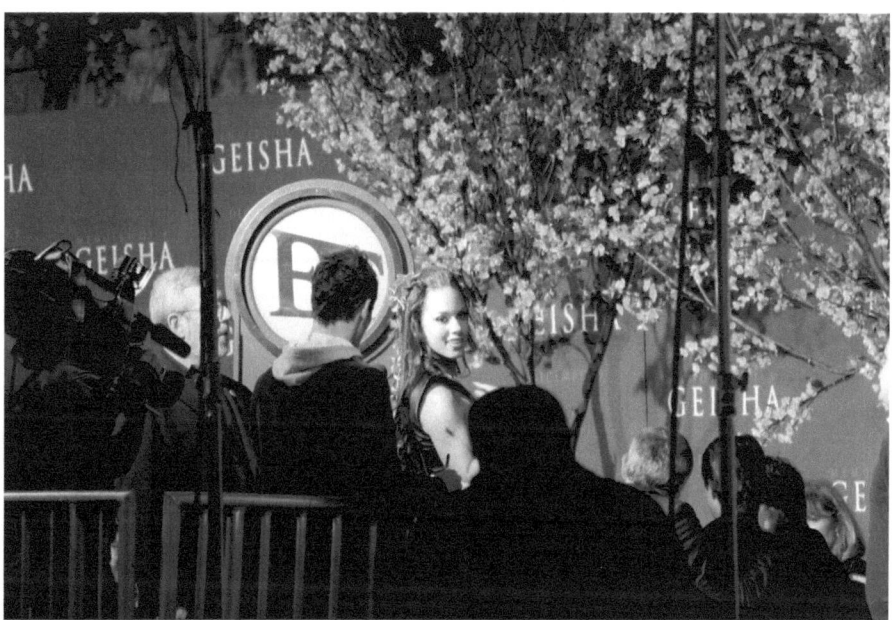

Getting shots of famous people can be difficult and a good telephoto lens can help

After using the Canon GL-2 for a few years I sold it and got a Canon XH-A1 high definition camcorder that I have also enjoyed very much. But like the tiny pocket still cameras there are many small and inexpensive camcorders available, many that are also high definition, that will do a wonderful job of helping you create fabulous family movies or movies for just about any purpose you want.

Video Uses

There's almost no limit to the number of uses we can find for the videos we take of ourselves, friends, family, co-workers and on and on. And possibly the most popular use is simply doing the videos just for all the fun we get to have with it. Decades ago we had to take the movie, send it away in the mail and wait a few weeks to get the film back so we could watch it. Those were the good old days when few people even had a video camera, and probably only really wealthy people had one with sound. Now days a camcorder is almost a standard household item, especially for people who have those cute kids with all the adorable expressions and actions that we want to capture for an eternity.

A lot of us have a good time while we make a short video to post on our social networking site to keep our friends and family up to date about our activities. Sites like FaceBook and YouTube can lend hours of enjoyment to us and our friends when we so easily upload our videos. If we want to spend a little more time we can make an instructional video about how to cook some of our favorite recipes, or share with others our crafts and hobbies. Your camcorder might be small and compact enough to take it with you just about anywhere you go, making it convenient to capture some party fun or any number of social engagements, not to mention keeping it running a good part of the time when you are enjoying that special vacation that you have dreamed about for years and want to keep forever in videos.

No matter for what purpose we use our videos it's not at all difficult to improve the quality of them and take them to the next level of fun by following a few basic rules.

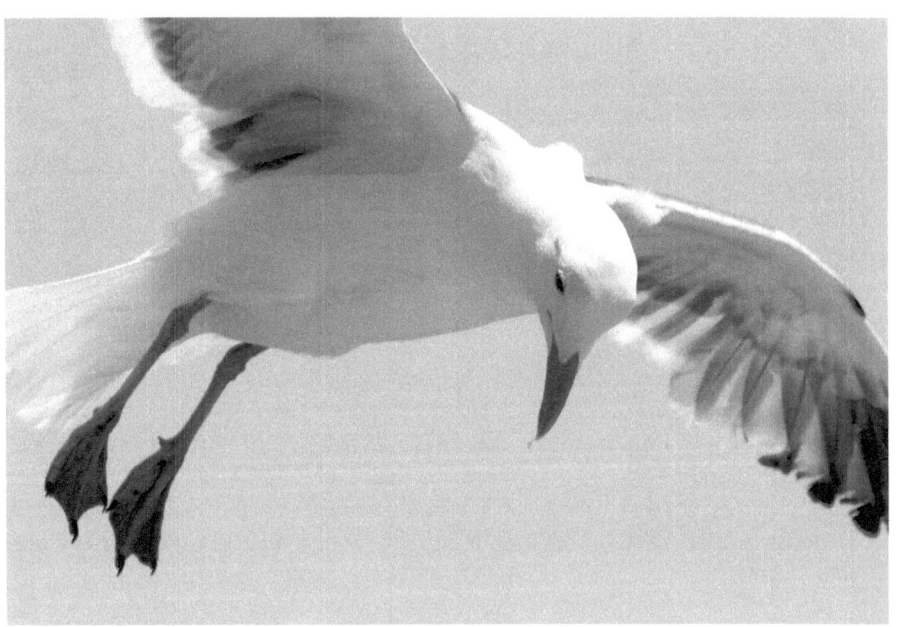

Video Basics

The basics for taking good video are pretty much the same as for your still photos, distance, lighting, distractions in the scene etc., except that it takes a little more stamina on the part of the photographer, since you spend much more time taking the video than you do when taking still shots. A tripod can be of help in some situations but may not be necessary if your camcorder has the image stabilization feature. When shooting indoors the lighting can be even more of a key factor for many camcorders particularly if you are shooting in HD (high definition).

Camcorder Settings

Most camcorders have a number of settings such as auto, night, action and so forth. For most purposes the auto setting will be your best bet particularly if you don't want to get into more complicated things with the aperture setting, shutter speed etc. Auto is easier unless you would like to experiment with the more technical aspects of your camcorder, which can be quite interesting and fun.

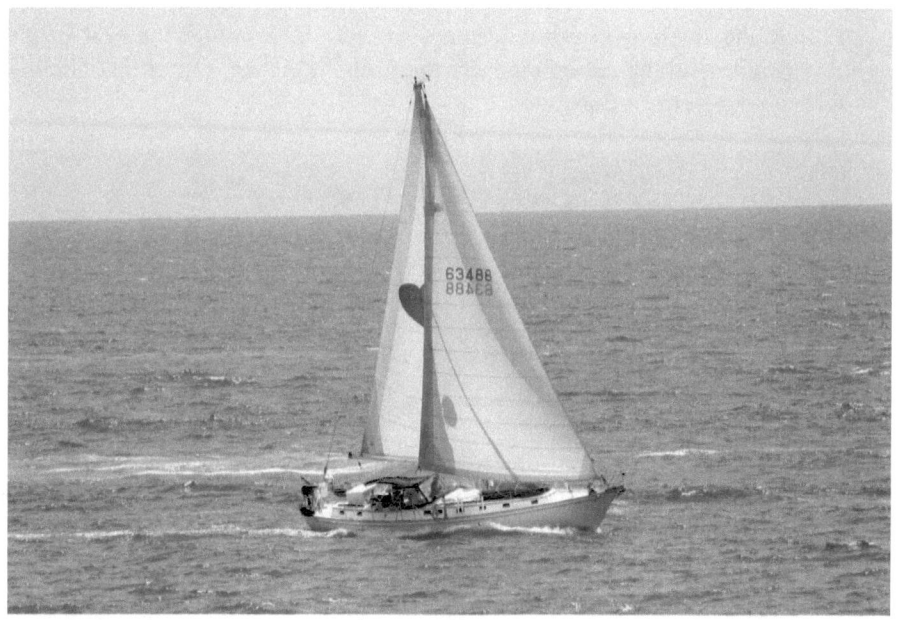

Lighting Check

Just a few minutes of preparation before you begin to film your movie can mean a big difference in the results. It's a good idea to do a lighting check by filming a short sample for a few seconds and play it back to see how the sample looks. If the lighting doesn't look good you might want to use a night setting, if your camera has that. Otherwise the auto mode will be fine. As with still shots making your film can be improved by using indirect lighting rather than having strong spotlights or floodlights aimed directly at your subjects. Bouncing the light off a wall or ceiling can be bright enough for good quality and provide a softer and more attractive look to your video.

Extra Photo Lights - Floodlights

Whatever your type of camera it has a built in flash that probably does a fine job on most occasions. Indoors or out, we can optionally use extra lighting in order to improve the quality of our photos, such as floodlights or a flash device or devices that are external to our camera. Extra lighting can be quite helpful in eliminating unwanted shadow from the subject(s).

Many cameras have a connection on top that will allow for attaching an extra flash device, and some also have a connection available for plugging in with one or more external flash devices. The external flash devices can be positioned at various points and aimed at our subjects and will be triggered by the camera when we press the button, providing the desired additional lighting to get the best results. If we experiment a little with the external flash devices by pointing them at a wall or ceiling, we may find we get the best results by bouncing the additional lighting off the walls or ceiling, rather than aiming the light directly at our subjects.

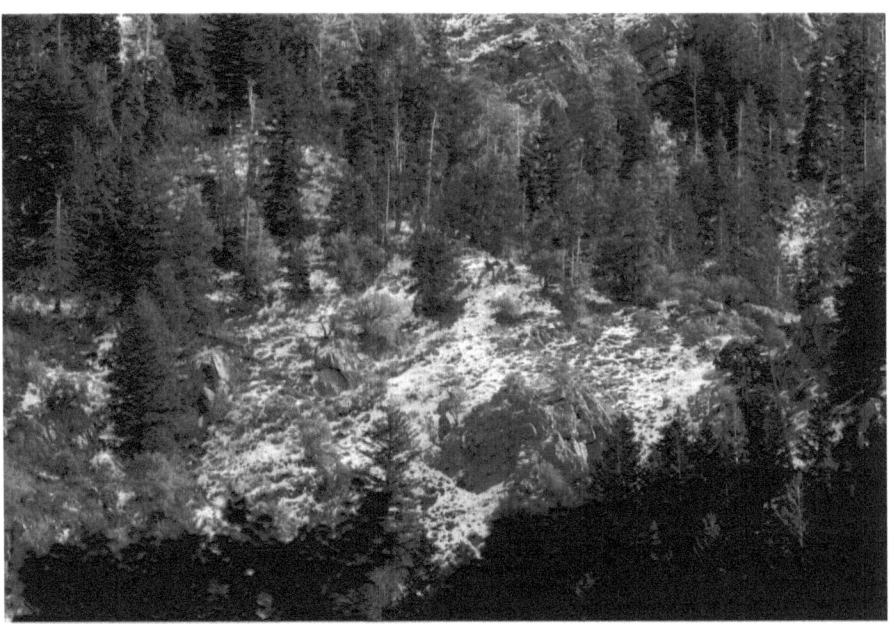

Photography stores have an almost unlimited number of accessory items available for our use, of which lighting stands and lights are among them. You may have seen lights mounted on stands with an umbrella around the light. The umbrellas that are portable and can be placed anywhere provide a softening effect to the lighting.

The better camcorders for video also have a built in light or have attachments for connecting a light, that enable us to get a better quality video with some extra light on the subjects.

Sound Check

The sound from your movie can mean the difference between it being an excellent video or an amateur video. Having the sound blasting at full volume or so low that it cannot be heard can be quite annoying and so distracting the video that no one will even want to finish watching it. Doing a sound check to make sure you have a good steady sound level throughout the entire video at an acceptable volume will make a major difference in the overall desire to view your entire video.

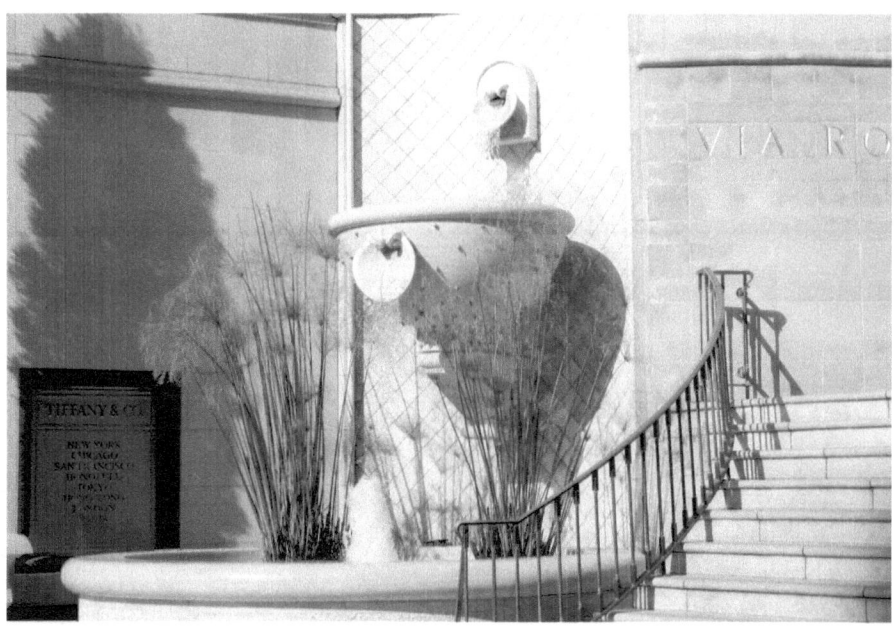

You don't have to be making a major motion picture to appreciate a steady sound level throughout your movie. A stable sound level will add a lot of quality to your movie and avoid the annoying thing of having to adjust the sound when you are playing it back. If your camcorder has a sound level adjustment or volume attenuation control it's good to do a sound check prior to starting your filming, then be sure not to change the sound level after you start filming. Keep it as uniform as possible throughout the entire video.

The same is true if using a still camera with sound to make your movie. It could be that your camera will adjust the sound automatically for you. But if there is a sound level meter on it, do a check prior to shooting to ensure you get as uniform a sound level as possible throughout your entire movie. Set the sound level to about three quarters of maximum and you should be fine, unless you are in an environment where the sound is very loud, like a party, then you may want to set your sound level to about half of maximum.

Microphones

For most purposes the built-in microphone that comes with your camcorder or camera will do quite well. If you like to experiment and want to get a bit fancy and spend some money you can look into directional microphones. A directional microphone is external to your camcorder, mounts on the camcorder in some cases, or mounts on a stand off to the side, and will focus on the sound coming from your subject and minimize sounds from surrounding areas.

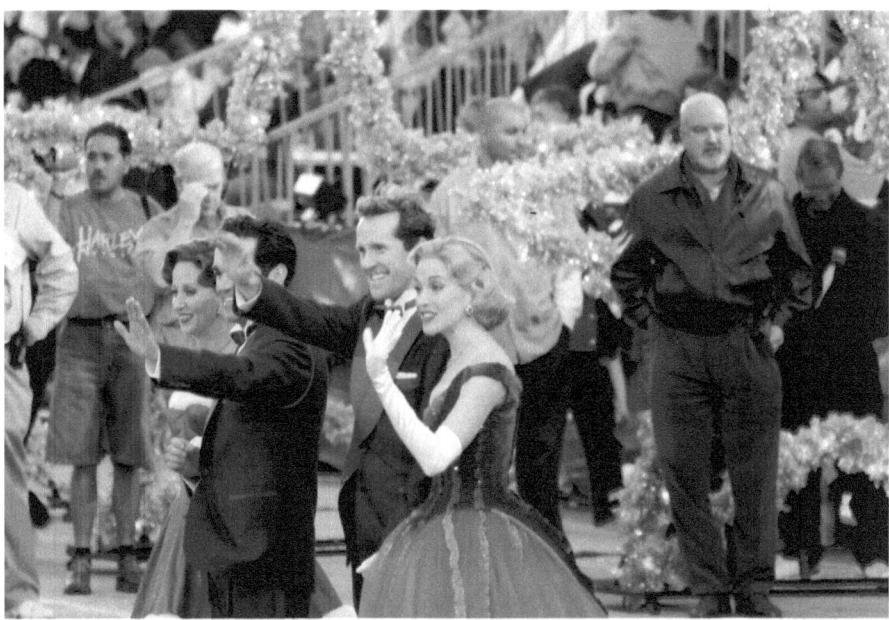

If you happen to be making a training video with someone speaking, your camcorder's microphone will do fine, but you can get more professional results with a Lavalier microphone, that is external, connected to the camera and attaches to the collar, lapel or pocket of the person who is speaking for hands free use. Examples of Lavalier microphones are those used by TV announcers that catch mostly the sounds of the announcer and minimize all other sounds.

CHAPTER SIX

Video Editing Software

As with taking still photos you can save yourself a lot of editing work by taking the best footage possible that will need the least amount of editing. For example, it can take a little practice to develop the habit, but when you are taking some footage and can see someone or something about to come in front of your lense that you do not want in the video, you can press your pause button, rather than thinking, "oh, I will just edit that out later."

You will find that pressing the pause button at the right times can save you tons of editing time and work. But that's when you see the obstruction coming toward your scene. When you don't see the unwanted coming into your scene, and all of a sudden your scene is mostly the back of someone's head, you have no choice and have to do your editing. But by keeping this in mind you can save yourself a lot of editing time by using the pause button when able to do so.

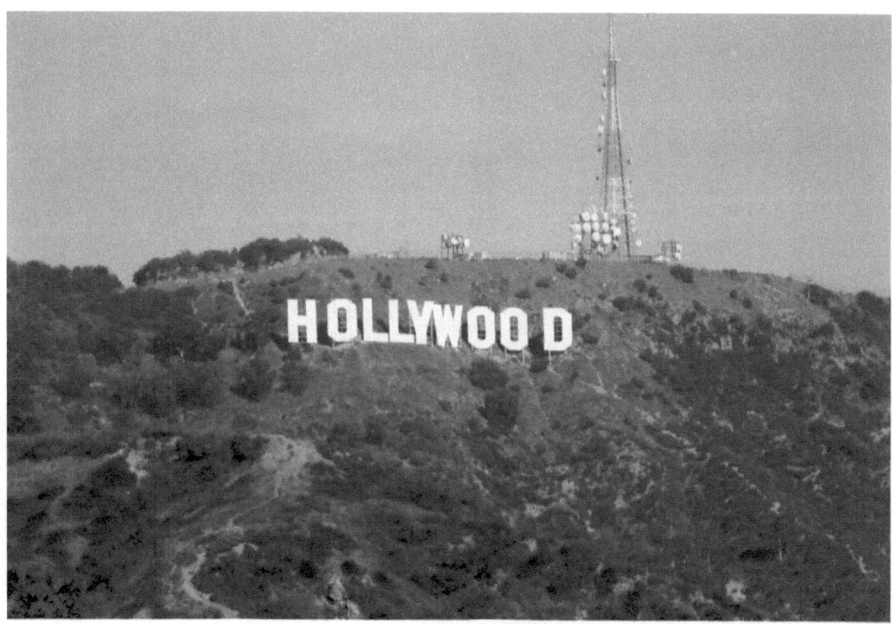

As to what kind of software to use for editing, many of the camcorders on the market come with some kind of free video editing software, or maybe a light trial version. If yours didn't come with software for editing your movies there is probably a low-cost or free solution for your editing needs. An excellent source online for low-cost or free software is Cnet's Download.com at http://download.Cnet.com/windows/.

To transfer the video files from your camcorder to your computer you may need to get what's known as a 1394 Fire Wire card to put into your computer, unless your camcorder will allow you to load your movies onto your computer with the standard USB transfer mode. If you need something like this you can likely find it by doing a search on sites such as Tech Depot at http://www.techdepot.com/pro/default.asp?stchg=1.

If you use a Mac computer there may be some editing software that came with the operating system on your machine. If not in the help system on your Mac there should be some suggestions as to where you can get the software. I have never used a Mac but understand they are a little more money but are worth it for the advantages offered.

If you use Windows XP there is Windows Movie Maker that comes free with most versions of XP. It's unlikely that your PC with XP does not include Windows Movie Maker, but it is possible since there are different versions of the XP operating system. If Movie Maker was not included in your version of Windows XP, you will find that it is no longer available for download from the Microsoft websites, and has been replaced on Windows 7 with Windows Live Movie Maker.

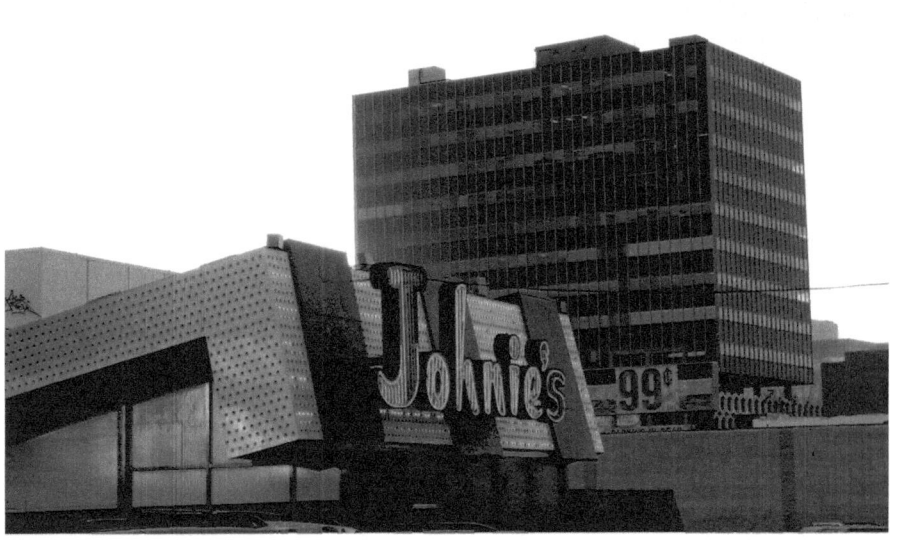

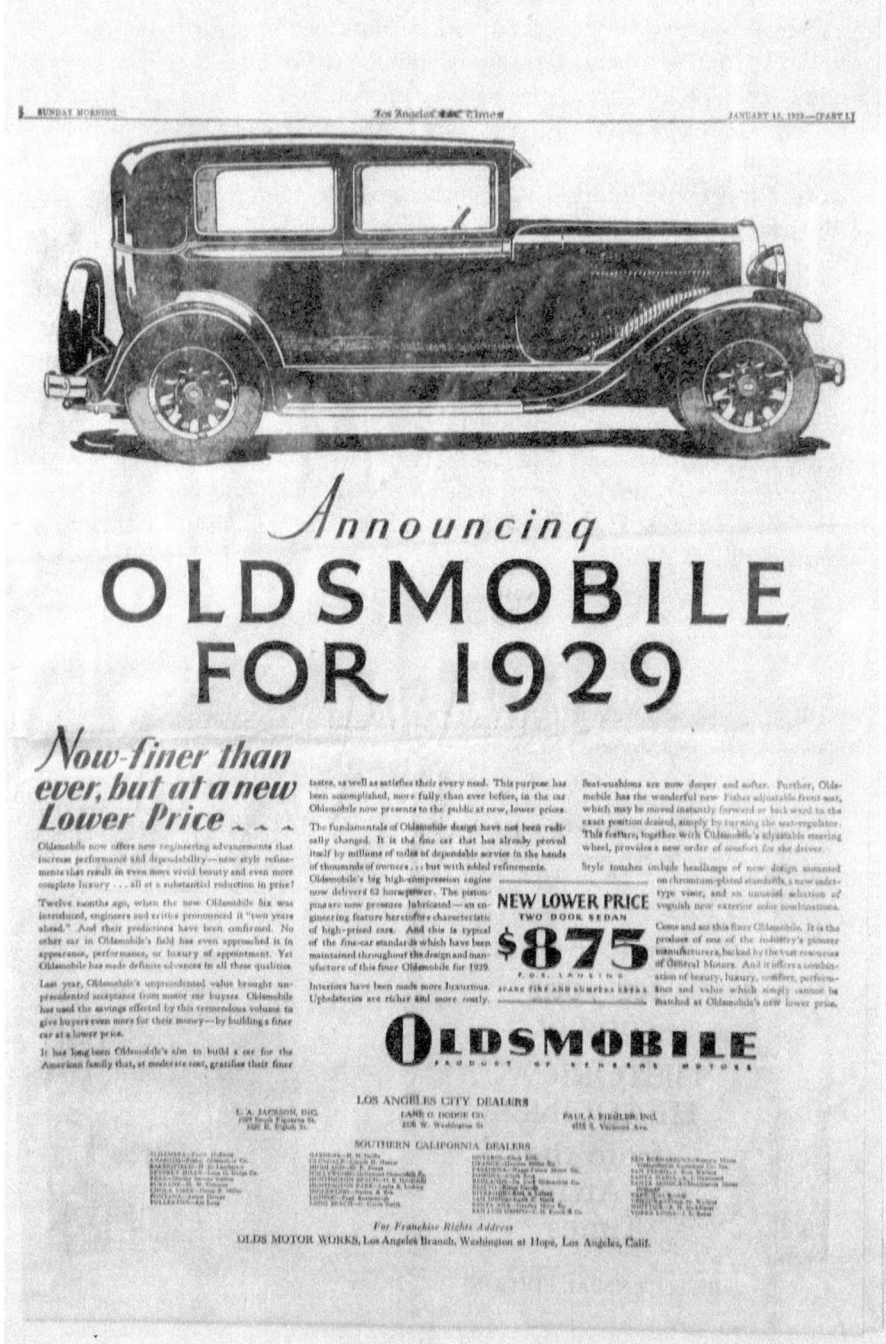

Yes, that's such a good price! I'll take it. Please wrap it up for me!

Although it is being discontinued Windows Movie Maker for Windows XP will be around for a few years, as long as people continue using the XP operating system, and has many useful features that will allow you to quickly and easily enhance your videos with a more professional look. You can add music, narration, scene transitions, titles, credits and the like, as well as a number of special effects such as slow motion and so forth. It's your choice as to how fancy you want to make your video. Keeping it simple is probably the best, with a title page, credits at the end and maybe some music. A few enhancements are find but too much elaborate editing can be distracting from the main theme of your video.

Windows Live Movie Maker that comes free with Windows 7 does quite a good job for most general purposes. It's quick and easy to use with some attractive features for making your home movies very presentable to family, friends or co-workers. It allows users to add attractive items such as a title page at the beginning, scene transitions and credits at the end. Your movies can be burned onto a CD or DVD or uploaded onto your favorite websites. If you have been using Windows Movie Maker for XP don't be surprised if your movie files cannot be edited with Windows Live. In this case you will need to load your videos again onto the Windows 7 operating system, in order to edit them.

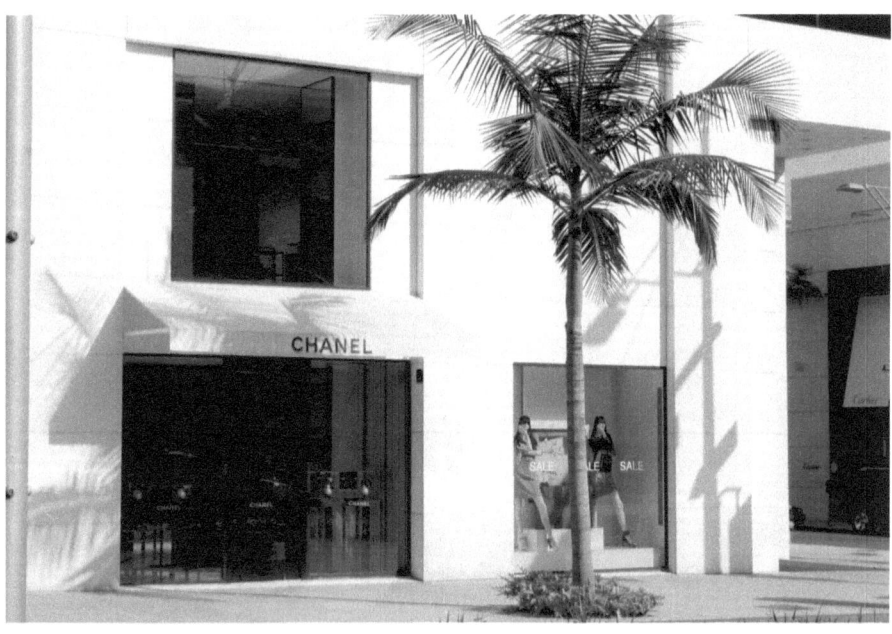

Windows Movie Maker for Windows XP and Windows Live Movie Maker for Windows 7 are both free and very useful. If you would like to get into a bit more advanced video editing there are a number of other video editing types of software available.

For less than $100 you can get Roxio Creator which includes MyDVD for creating and editing movies with about the best quality possible. There is Roxio Creator 2009 that works very well with a lot of additional programs as well, if you are using Windows XP. If your operating system is Windows 7 you will have to purchase Roxio Creator 2010. If you find that Roxio Creator 2010 does not work on Windows 7, you can contact their support department for help in resolving the problem. If you're using Windows 7 you can do fine with Windows Live Movie Maker as a basic program, as long as you use windows AVI files and not Mpeg files. You can use either type of file but AVI is much easier to edit. Using the Mpeg files is more difficult since the editing process is slower than with the AVI files.

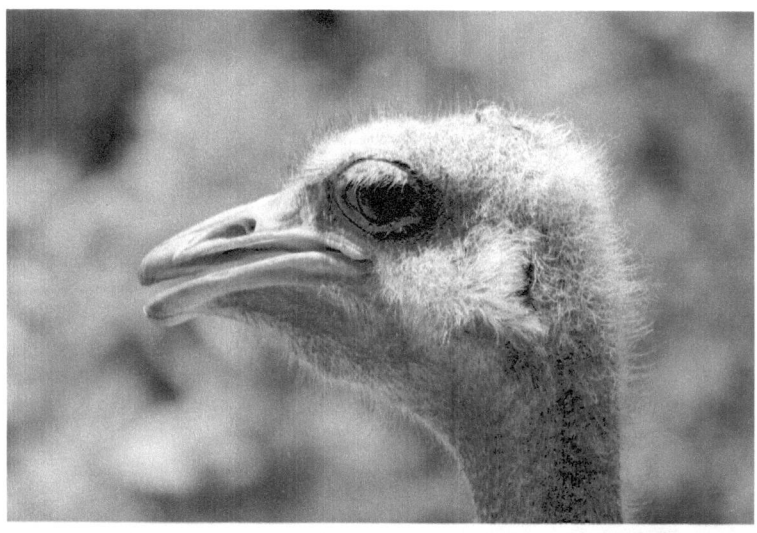

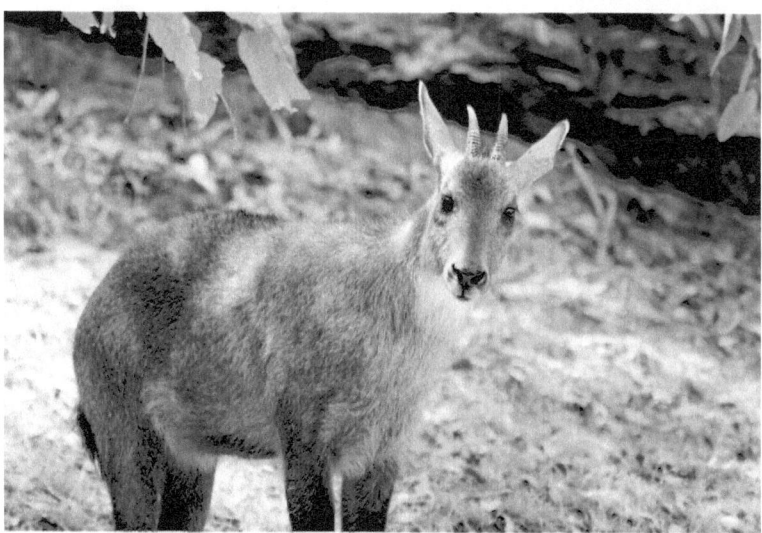

CHAPTER SEVEN

Aerial Photography – Can You Imagine?

This isn't for everybody particularly if everybody has a fear of heights or gets airsickness, but for the rest of us, if there is anything more fun that taking pictures or moving pictures it's taking them from somewhere in the sky.

You don't have to be a photographer for a production company that is making a major motion picture in order to enjoy many of the thrills of aerial photography. And the best way to get excellent shots or some very good footage for a movie is by shooting from a helicopter. Most major airports and general aviation airports have companies that will rent a helicopter and pilot to you for an hour or so, while you take your photos or a movie. It's not cheap but can be well worth the money depending upon how much interest you have in getting some good shots. You can plan on a few hundred dollars per person for an hour flight.

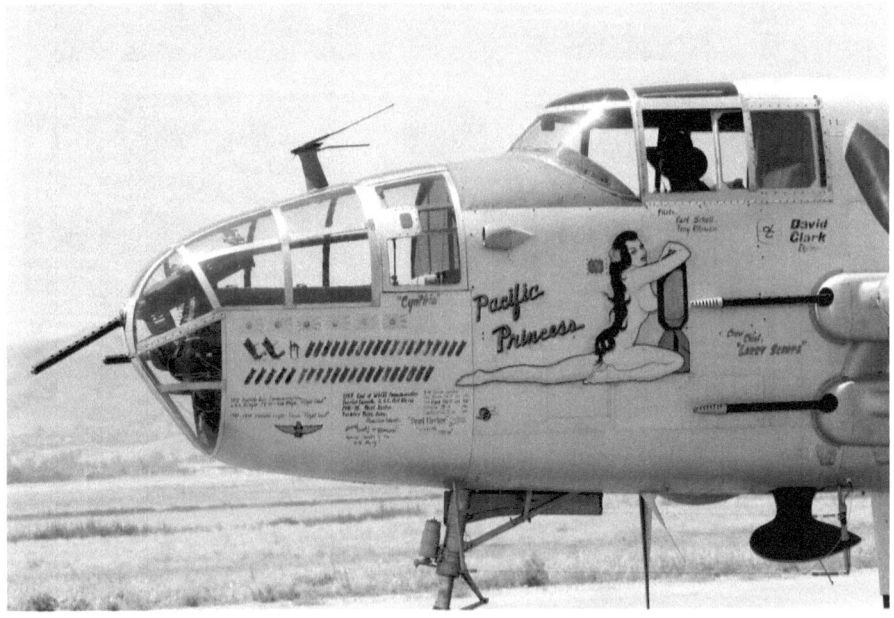

In 2004 I chartered a helicopter for an hour flight at Corporate Helicopters located at Montgomery Field in San Diego. They are a few miles north of Lindbergh Field or San Diego International Airport. The pilot was a very nice girl by the name of Elizabeth, and as are most pilots she was quite polite, friendly and cordial. It was a small two-seat rotor helicopter, the bubble type where you can see everything through the bubble. It was a Robinson SR-22 model. It was a fun ride. Even with the best weather in August at eighty degrees and sunny, you get a bit of a slight bumpy ride in the small rotor ships because of light turbulent winds, but it was nothing at all disturbing or distracting.

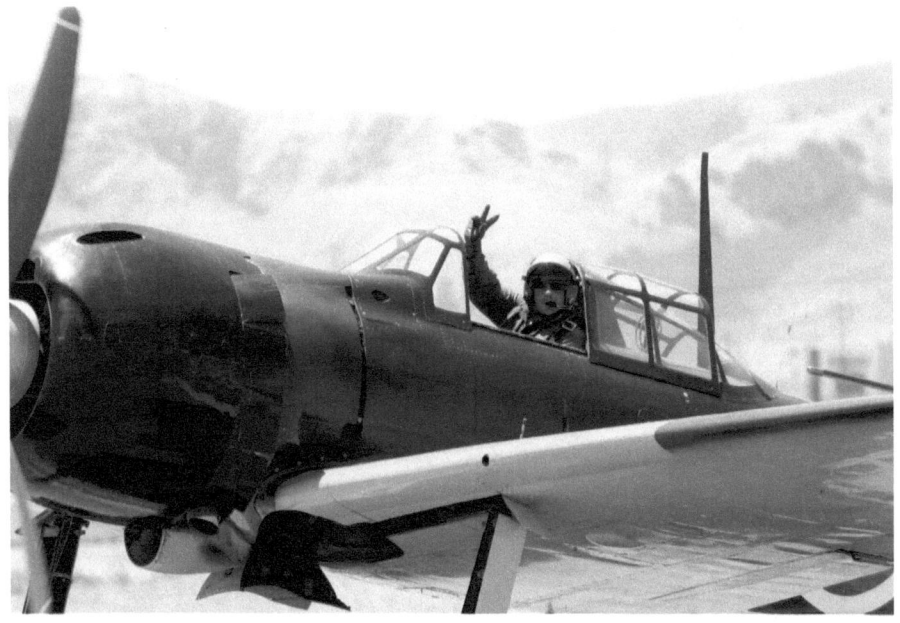

We left Montgomery Field, leveled off at 1,600 feet and headed north going over the Miramar Marine Corps Air Station and saw an FA-18 fighter jet passing over the field. A left turn took us toward the ocean where we made another left that took us south along the sea coast of San Diego and La Jolla. It was some of the best scenery anyone could ever imagine. There is a short several minute sample video of some of it posted on YouTube at http://www.youtube.com/watch?v=CDntUsuUCxo, and the complete 40 minute movie is available from one of my websites at http://www.airshowmovies.net

I took a few still shots with my Canon GL-2 but most the hour was spent filming the video. We proceeded south along the coastline past the very beautiful area of La Jolla, did a circle over Sea World, went over Lindbergh Field and Downtown San Diego, then we headed back toward our starting point at Montgomery Field.

The footage I got did not include sound except for the first minute or so of the video when she was warming up the engine, after which I turned the sound off. We were flying with the door off on my side so I could get the best shots, and the noise from the wind and helicopter blades would have been quite annoying.

The pilot was good. She did a very nice job of keeping in touch with the tower and other aircraft in the vicinity, to make sure everybody knew our location at all times. She made small talk with me as well, which most pilots will do, since part of their job is selling flying lessons to people who like to fly. I probably seemed a little rude to her when she was making small talk, with my eyes on the camcorder's viewfinder most the time as I was taking footage of the fabulous seashore and coastline 800 feet below us.

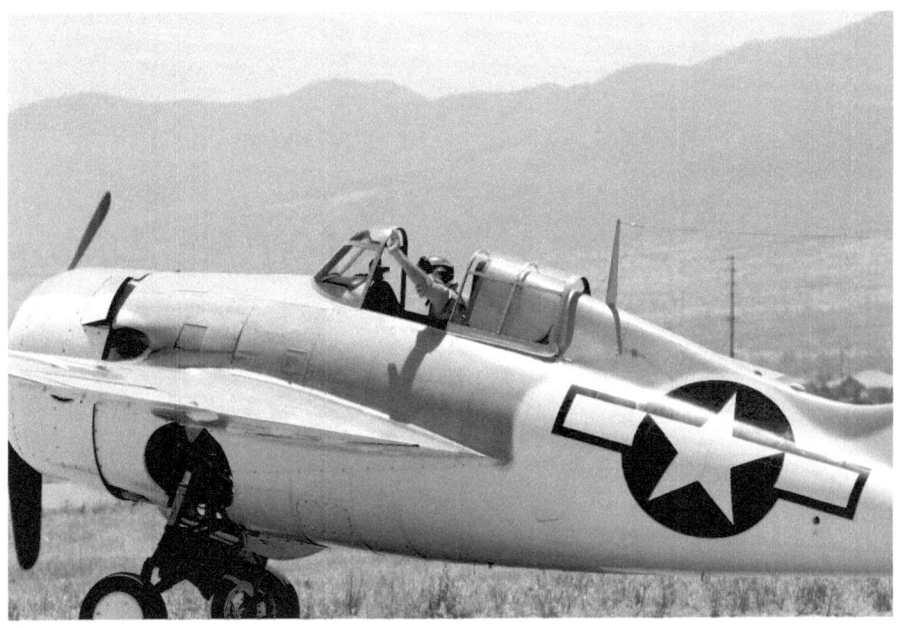

There was no problem with her talking to me, other than the fact that she was getting ignored a lot. When she talked with me it was through the intercom connected to our headsets. But when she talked with other aircraft or the tower it was on the radio of course, and the powerful radiation from the radio caused a problem with the circuit board in my camera. I didn't realize the camera had been damaged until some time after the flight when I notice that the zoom no longer worked. The helicopter radio had damaged the digital camera's circuits. I knew this was the case because when I played back the tape I could here the pilot talking on her radio, and the camcorder had it's sound level turned all the way down.

There probably would have been no damage had I been using one of the older film cameras, or had we been in a larger helicopter with more shielding between the radio beams and the camera. But fortunately my camcorder was under warranty. I sent it in for service and was overjoyed to get it back a week later as good as new. When I played the tape back there were a lot of parts that had to be edited out, where the zoom had gone crazy and zoomed all the way in, stuff like that. But I managed to salvage about 40 minutes of good footage.

So if you decide to do some photography from a small aircraft, and are using a digital camcorder or maybe even a digital small camera of some kind, you may want to wrap some tinfoil for shielding around your camera while in that small aircraft to protect your camera from the radio beams. Using a precaution like this may not at all be necessary. It could be that most aircraft provide a better shielding factor between the radio antenna and your camera, but the fact is it can and did happen to me. And it won't hurt anything at all to take the precautionary measures with your beloved camera.

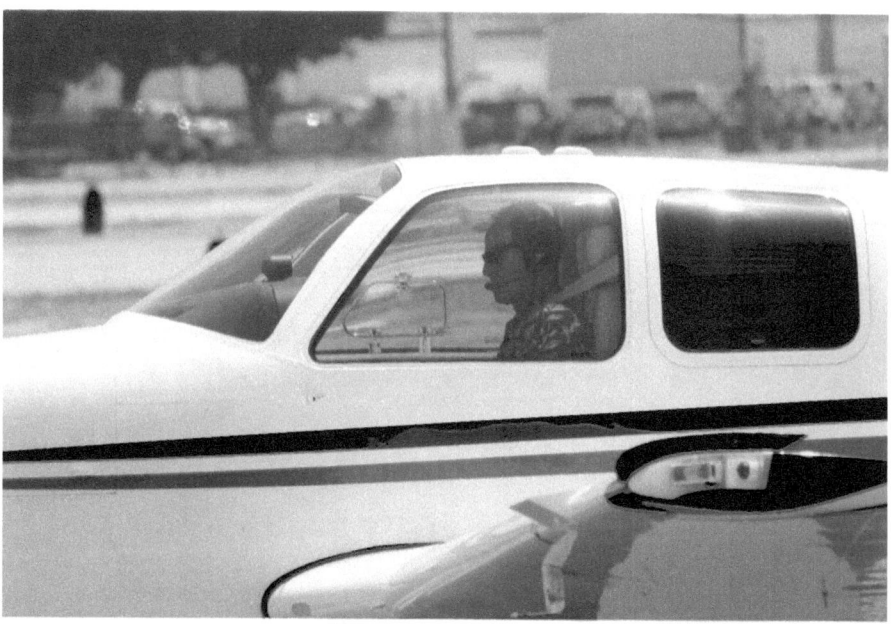

Just about any kind of aircraft would be fun for flight, but helicopters tend to be more accommodating for getting the best views and capturing them with your cameras.

Even if you don't want to get photographs or videos while on a flight, photographing all the different kinds of planes while on the ground at a small airport as they land and take off can be a lot of fun.

CHAPTER EIGHT

The Joys Of A Telephoto Lens

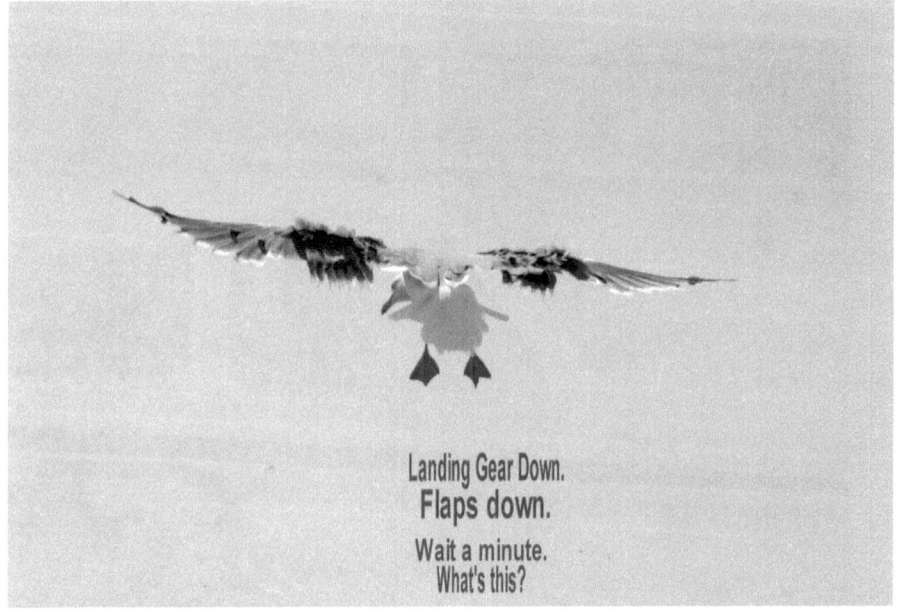

Landing Gear Down.
Flaps down.
Wait a minute.
What's this?

Many of the small pocket cameras have a zoom function on the lens that can help in getting better shots. If you happen to have one of the larger cameras you may be fortunate if you have the capability to use interchangeable lenses. This is one of the advantages of using a camera that is a little more advanced than most of the small pocket cameras with fixed lenses. If you are able to take your regular lens off and put on a telephoto lens, you will be able to get some incredibly nice distance shots that you would not be able to get with your regular lens.

A telephoto lens is particular good if you like getting shots of scenery, wildlife and many other outdoor subjects. And they are also very nice if you are at an event of some kind and would like to get a shot of a famous person, a movie premier for example, where you are quite a distance from your subject and need a good zoom. The sample shots below were all taken with a telephoto lens on my Canon Rebel XT.

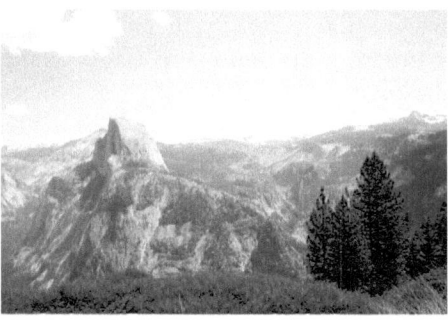

All the shots you see here were taken with the Canon Rebel XT with a EF70-300mm lens f/4-5.6 IS USM. Yes, that's a lot of numbers to think about, and will not mean anything unless you become familiar with the different lenses that are available.

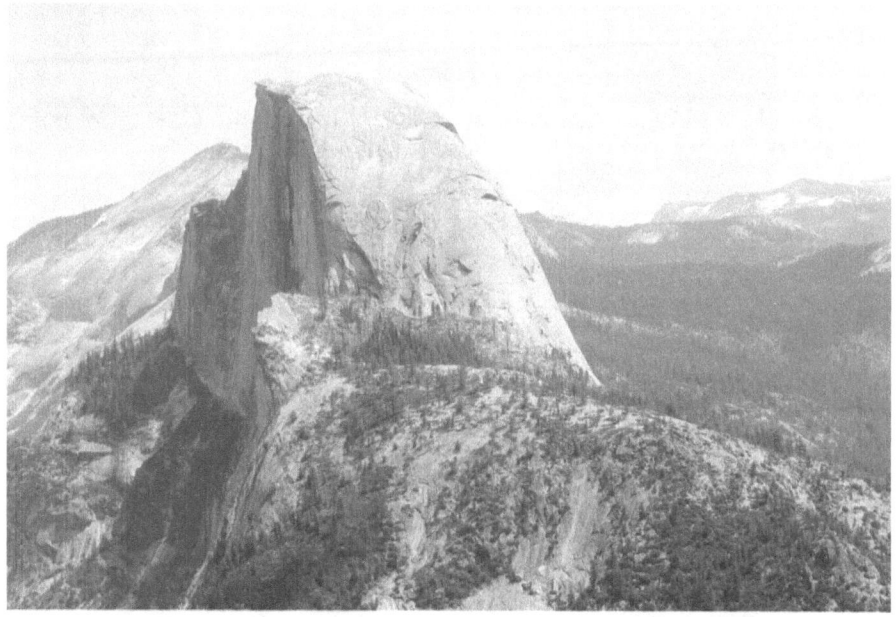

A problem with telephoto lenses is that when zoomed all the way in on your subject, depending upon your type of camera you may find it difficult to keep the camera steady enough to get a shot that is not blurred.

The very nice thing about most or all of the Canon interchangeable lenses is that they work with the camera in focusing and freezing the image just before you take the shot. There is an adjustment on this lens for switching between taking shots of still scenery or subjects that are moving. You can spend a lot on lenses depending upon what you want to do. This lense was about $750.00, nearly as much as the cost of the camera.

The two shots above are different shots of the same subject taken with the same telephoto lens, Half Moon at Yosemite National Park. The first shot was taken with the zoom all the way out, the second zoomed all the way in.

It's interesting that the manufacturers of the telephoto lenses rate them in millimeters, the length that the lens extracts, rather than the power of the zoom, such as 10X zoom or 20X zoom, like we see camcorder zoom lenses rated. But no matter how they are rated it's just nice to know they work so well and enable us to get shots that we could in no way get without them.

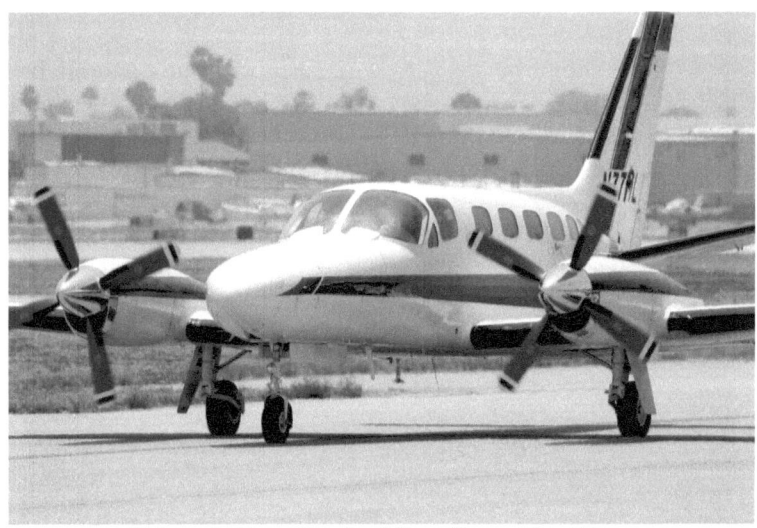

Taken A Few Hundred Feet From The Plane

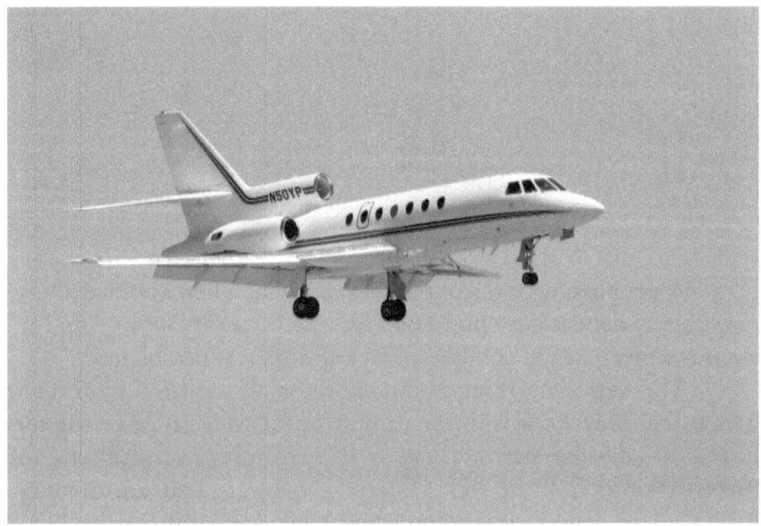

Taken About A Half Mile From The Plane

Telephoto lenses can cost in the thousands of dollars but you can save a lot by doing some shopping around. And you don't have to get the most expensive lens in order to get some fabulous shots. It's best to study and learn about them before buying to make sure you get what you need at as good a price as possible.

The telephoto lenses for camcorders are very nice as well, but you would do well with staying with not more than a 20 to 40 power zoom. That is really all you need to get good footage. Using any more power than that might require a tripod even if your camcorder has image stabalization. I have used my Canon GL-2 camcorder with a lens that was rated at up to 100X but it was hard to steady the camera at 100X zoom. I found that 20 to 40 power in most instances did quite a good job and it was much easier to keep the camcorder steady.

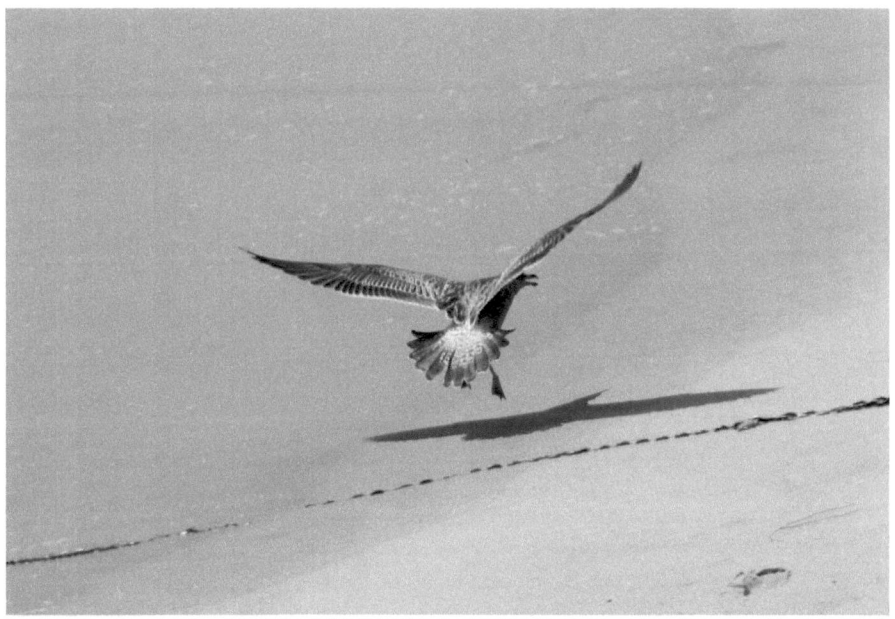

As much as many of us like the small pocket cameras we don't always realize there can be quite a difference in them and the cameras that cost a little more. It's more than just paying for the name brand when getting a camera that's somewhat more sophisticated. We might find things like less blur with many of our action photos. There is a reason for all the settings on the cameras that cost more. It's fine to use the small pocket cameras for general purpose, and not worry about those settings on the more expensive cameras. But it's good to know for those of us who want to take it to the next level we can do so without spending too much more in order to get the best shots possible.

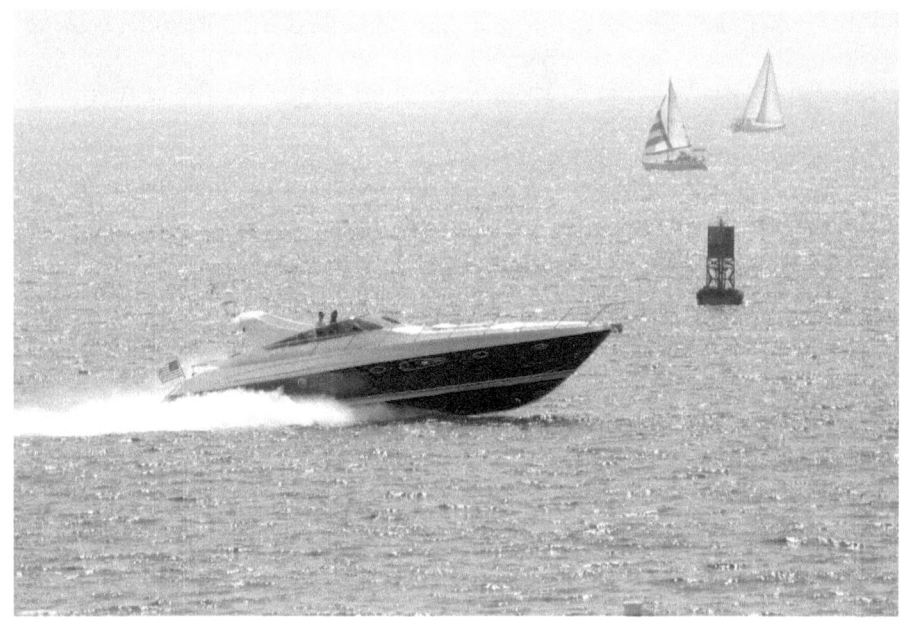

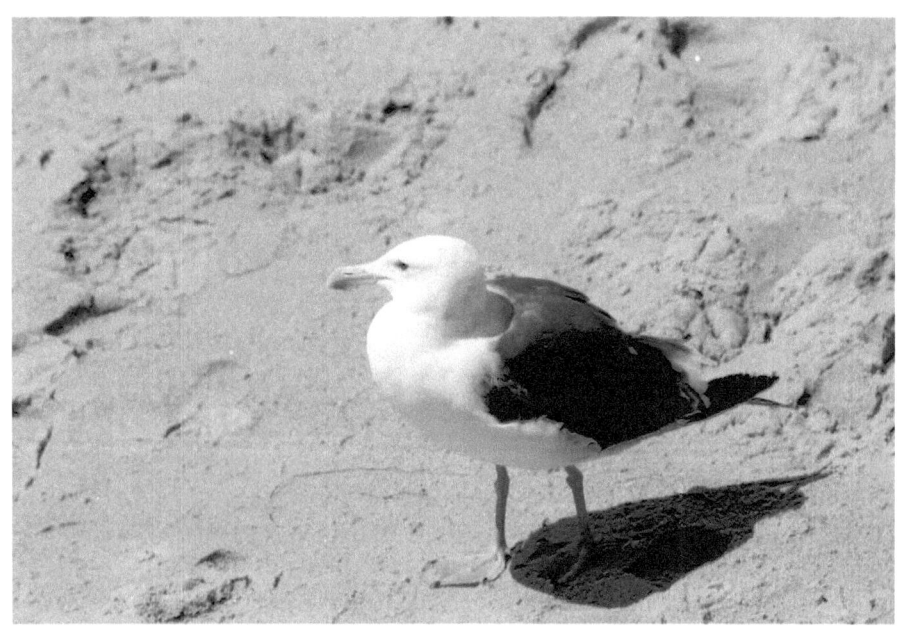

CHAPTER NINE

Should I Become A Professional?

After having so much fun taking photos and videos, and learning simple ways of making them better, many of us might get the thought of how nice it would be to do something like this for a living. Making money doing what we like most seems like it would be about as good as it could get.

A question you may have already asked yourself is, "why would anyone want to become a professional these days with almost everybody having a camera? Who needs a professional photographer?" The fact is there are probably more opportunities today for professional photographers than ever before. Although most people do have at least one of the small pocket cameras they are used mostly for personal use. You will find that many people who use the small personal cameras will still hire a professional photographer for the best in family portraits. And there are also many kinds of professional photography.

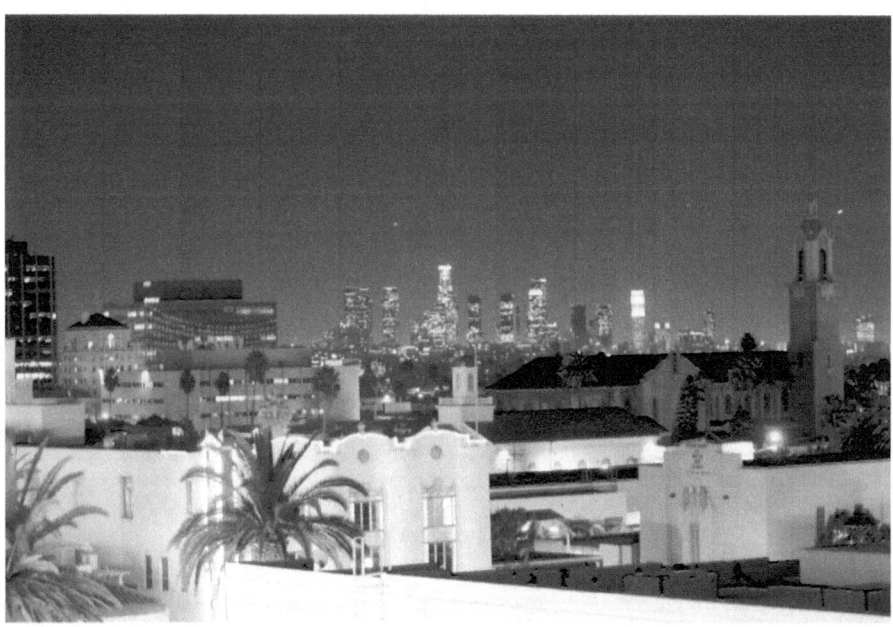

TV stations, newspapers and news companies, just to mention a few, always have a need for good photographers. Of course, a career in photography is best preceded by some good education the subject, which is readily available for anyone who has the desire and wants to make the commitment. Even if you don't plan on becoming a professional there are many schools and classes available that you might find exciting and most beneficial. If someone wants to be a professional and would like to work on their own, there are lots of opportunities for the independent photo buffs.

With the coming about of the advancements in digital photography, this just makes it better. More people have access to excellent equipment than ever before. The horror movie, Paranormal Activity, was made into a major motion picture for the ridiculously low budget of only $15,000.00. The movie was released in 2009 with production that started on it in 2007. In just a few weeks after the opening of the movie it had grossed something like sixty-two million dollars. In prior years the cost of the camera itself to film the movie may have cost more than $15,000.00. With the technology now available at such lower prices the possibilities are staggering.

But I could never be that good, you may tell yourself. Well, think again, because probably the major difference between an amateur golfer, ball player, photographer or anything else is the amount of practice they get.

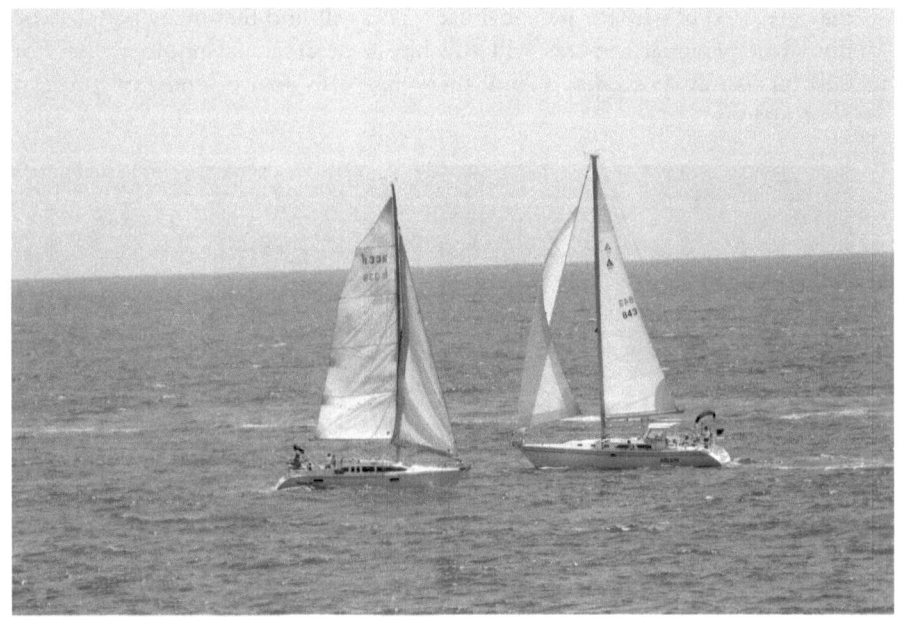

Legal Matters

What kinds of things are legal to photograph? Can I take photos of anything I want, and use them for any purpose I want? No, not really, but you do have a lot of latitude. You can take photos and videos of just about anything you would like, if your photos and videos are for your own personal use, to enjoy for yourself and maybe share with your friends and family. But if you use your photography for commercial purposes there certainly are restrictions that do apply.

Taking photos and videos of famous people to make money can be quite exciting and lucrative, but it can also be very dangerous as well. The celebrities may not like having you take their picture and may appreciate some privacy and consideration even when they are out and in the public eye. Taking photos or video of celebrities at a movie premier would be quite acceptable, and even expected, but you may want to ask yourself if you would like strangers taking shots of you when you are out at dinner or going to a movie. Just because so many people do it for money because it's legal does not mean that it's right. And there is now talk of legislation of some kind to put limits on the kinds of photos that can be taken of celebrities in some areas.

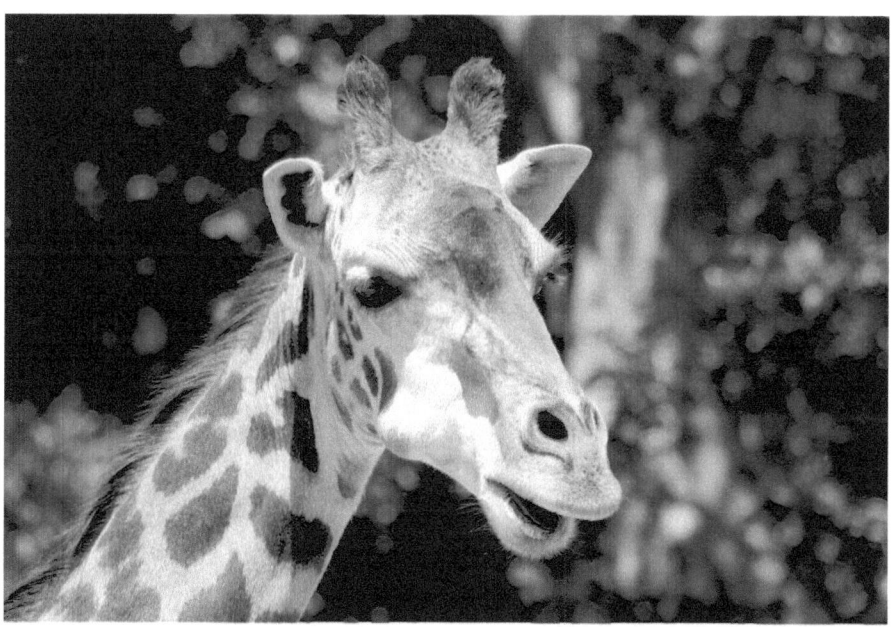

Taking photos of things that include trademarks of companies, for example, and selling the photos could likely be a problem. The companies that own the trademarks could complain and bring legal action. If taking pictures of famous people or scenes that include trademarks owned by someone else, a good rule to follow would be considerate by first requesting permission before taking the photos or videos, or obtaining permission in writing prior to using the photos for any commercial purpose.

It's best to do a little research beforehand and find out what rules exist. For example, if you want to take photos and videos at an air show, you will find that some air shows are fine with it, while others have very strict rules that apply to any and all photography at "their" air show. If you were to be seen photographing at a major international airport, you would likely find yourself being detained by authorities and questioned about the purpose of your photos. If you photograph at a smaller general aviation airport it would probably not be problem in many cases, since many of the smaller airports and pilots like being photographed in support of general aviation, which has been a shrinking industry for some years.

Now matter how or where we get our photography, or what we use them for it's good to know a few basic principles that help us get the best photos possible.

Good luck and the very best of wishes to you in your photographic adventures.

Rex Lee Reynolds

About The Author

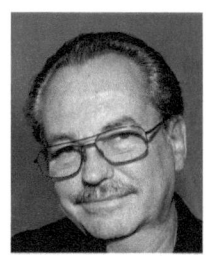

Rex Lee Reynolds has been writing books since the mid 1980ies, has written a dozen or so fiction and non-fiction books, and has published six books to date including this book, two fiction and four non-fiction. He has a number of other non-fiction books in the planning that are self-help books.

He is currently an engineer in the field of computer sciences, which began in 1995 with the development of WiseGuy InterActive Word Game for Kids and WiseGuy InterActive MathBox for Kids, still being distributed by www.digitalriver.com. He is also experienced in the fields of real estate, insurance, finance, healthcare, aviation and entertainment.

Most recent books published are Checklist For Publishing & Selling Your Books in Janurary 2010, June of 2009 are Trouble in Sleepy Springs, suspense crime mystery and Closet Full of Teddy Bears, romantic situation comedy stories. These books are published in print and e-book by LuLu Publishing at www.lulu.com and are available at www.lulu.com and www.amazon.com.

Rex is a professional photographer, owns and manages two businesses, a modeling and talent agency at www.momentsofmagicphoto.com and an airplane enthusiast movie business at www.airshowmovies.net.

Other Books By Rex Lee Reynolds

Rex Lee Reynolds is a featured author at www.authorsden.com in the categories of Action/Thriller, Education/Training, Humor and Publishing. His other books are available in print and e-book from www.amazon.com and www.lulu.com and include,

Checklist For Publishing & Selling Your Books – 2010
Closet Full Of Teddy Bears – Humor – 2009
Trouble In Sleepy Springs – Action/Thriller – 2009

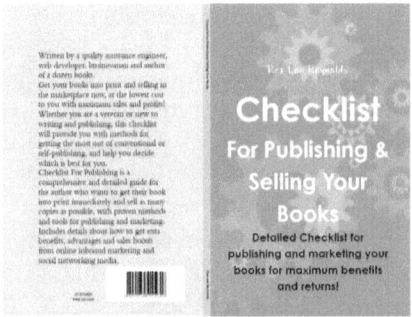

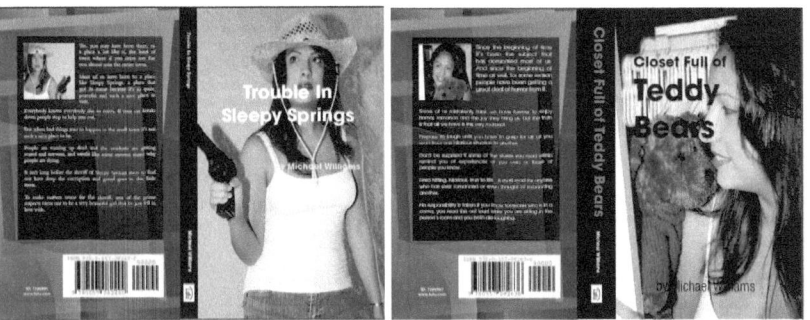

Index

accessory items, 40
aerial photography, 48
artistic effect, 14
auto mode, 39
background, 14, 15, 16, 17, 19
background junk, 16
backup copies, 26
bad mood, 18
batteries, 29
Bell & Howell 8mm, 36
blurry, 15, 22, 23, 24
Bouncing the light, 39
camcorder, 9, 24, 25, 28, 29, 36, 37, 38, 39, 41, 42, 44, 50, 51, 54, 55
Canon GL-2, 37, 49, 55
CD, 4, 26, 29, 46
celebrities, 59
Cnet, 32, 44
Corel, 13, 32
Corporate Helicopters, 48
crystal clear, 16
direct sunlight, 14
distracting obstructions, 11, 31
Download.com, 32, 44
DVD, 4, 26, 29, 37, 46
editing software, 12, 14, 17, 32, 33, 35, 37, 43, 44
external disc, 26
external flash devices, 40
external hard drive, 26
Extreme temperatures, 28
face shadow, 12
family portraits, 57
famous people, 37, 59
film camera, 24
Fire Wire card, 44
flash, 11, 12, 14, 19, 21, 22, 25, 28, 40
flashcard, 29
Floodlights, 5, 21, 40
focus, 22, 42
free editing software, 32
Fuji Film J20, 10

general aviation, 48, 60
Happy Meals, 18
hard drives, 26
high definition, 9, 37, 39
horror movie, 58
ideal conditions, 12, 18
image stabilization, 24, 39
indirect lighting, 21, 39
instructional video, 38
Lavalier microphone, 42
legal to photograph, 58
lens, 10, 14, 22, 23, 24, 37, 52, 53, 54, 55
lighting, 10, 19, 21, 22, 31, 33, 38, 39, 40
lighting check, 39
Lindbergh Field, 48, 49
LuLu Publishing, 61
Mac computer, 44
Making money, 57
mega-pixels, 9, 37
memory, 10, 26, 29
memory card, 10
microphone, 42
moisture, 28
Montgomery Field, 48, 49
motion picture, 36, 41, 48, 58
movie camera, 24, 28, 36
MyDVD, 46
night photos, 23
night setting, 23, 39
night settings, 23
out of focus, 22
Paint Shop Pro, 13, 15, 32, 34
Paranormal Activity, 58
pause button, 43
photo editing, 15, 17, 32, 35
photo files, 26
photo shoot, 12, 17, 33, 34
Photo Shop, 15, 32
photo widow, 28
Photography indoors, 21
Photography stores, 40

pictures at night, 22
Pixels, 9
pocket cameras, 9, 10, 29, 52, 55, 57
police mug shots, 17
professional photographer, 6, 15, 57, 61
radio beams, 29, 50, 51
Raw Photo, 12, 14
Rebel XT, 9, 10, 52, 53
recording movies, 9
red eye prevention, 17
red eyes, 17
remote control, 24
rename files, 26
re-touched, 12, 13, 15, 33
Re-Touching, 4, 12, 32
Rex Lee Reynolds, 1, 2, 5, 60, 61, 62
Robinson SR-22, 49
Roxio Creator, 46
Roxio Creator 2009, 46
Roxio Creator 2010, 47
San Diego International, 48
self-portrait, 15
settings, 13, 23, 39, 55
shooting against the sun,, 11
shooting from a helicopter, 48
shots of yourself, 31
shutter speed, 23, 25, 39
simple rules, 9, 31

Single Lens Reflex, 22
SLRs, 22
Smart Photo Fix, 4, 13, 35
smoky conditions, 28
socially awkward, 22
softening effect, 40
sound check, 41
sound level, 41, 50
Special Lighting Effect, 20
specifications, 10
still shots, 25, 38, 39, 49
strap, 30
system resources, 26
tape drive, 29
tape re-winder, 29
Tech Depot, 44
telephoto lens, 52
Telephoto Lens, 5, 14, 35, 52
timed shots, 25
time-lapse, 25
tripod, 24, 25, 38, 55
umbrella, 40
USB transfer, 44
videotapes, 29
Windows 7, 44, 46, 47
Windows Live Movie Maker, 44, 46, 47
Windows Movie Maker, 44, 45, 46
Windows XP, 44, 45, 46, 47
XH-A1, 9, 37
zoom, 14, 24, 37, 50, 52, 54, 55

www.ingramcontent.com/pod-product-compliance
Lightning Source LLC
Chambersburg PA
CBHW021025180526
45163CB00005B/2126